ALSO BY DANIELLE KARTES

Rustic Joyful Food: My Heart's Table
Rustic Joyful Food: Generations
Rustic Joyful Food: Meant to Share

You Were Always There

NOTES *and* RECIPES *for* LIVING *a Life You* LOVE

DANIELLE KARTES

Published by Sourcebooks
P.O. Box 4410, Naperville, Illinois 60567-4410
(630) 961-3900
sourcebooks.com

Library of Congress Cataloging-in-Publication Data

Names: Kartes, Danielle, author.
Title: You were always there : notes and recipes for living a life you love / Danielle Kartes.
Description: Naperville, Illinois : Sourcebooks, [2022]
Identifiers: LCCN 2021042287 (print) | LCCN 2021042288 (ebook) | (trade paperback) | (epub)
Subjects: LCSH: Kartes, Danielle. | Restaurateurs--Washington (State)--Issaquah--Biography. | Women cooks--Washington (State)--Issaquah--Biography. | Cooks--Washington (State)--Issaquah--Biography.
Classification: LCC TX649.K37 A3 2022 (print) | LCC TX649.K37 (ebook) | DDC 647.95092 [B]--dc23
LC record available at https://lccn.loc.gov/2021042287
LC ebook record available at https://lccn.loc.gov/2021042288

Printed and bound in Canada.
MBP 10 9 8 7 6 5 4 3 2

For Mike & the boys

My Why

Introduction

I can still see a particular high school teacher of mine holding his hand out in front of himself twenty-two years ago, just an inch of space between his thumb and index finger. I was near graduation, about to enter the world I'd been told about for so long.

"You see," he said, "this time in your life feels big. It feels profound, and it is. But this time represents just this much of who you are meant to be and the life you've been created to live. This inch is just a moment in all your life, just a slice in the time you'll spend here. Make it worthwhile. Make it good. Never forget where you came from, and trudge ahead into this blessing of a life."

I invite you in to just an inch of *my* life, small yet profound, wrought with laughter and lessons and tears, cleansing words and honest truths I've learned, humble pie I've eaten, and glorious mountaintop moments, never to be forgotten. I have so much more to learn and live but so much to share.

These notes from my life encapsulate a time when I figured out that in spite of what I believed at the time, I had not lost myself. It presents a time in my life when my marriage, seemingly against the odds, survived and became a beautiful reminder to me of how much God truly cares about the smallest details, a time of forgiving myself and others. These essays paint a picture of building a business only to lose it all and then rebuilding a far more beautiful business in its place. I want to tell you things, like how I fell in love with my husband again after significant loss and how I fell in love with my life after it felt like my world was falling down around me. I want to tell you about my deep love for motherhood and the purpose I discovered in being a parent. I once thought food ruined my life, but in reality, it saved me. Cooking became my education, my therapy, my lifeline. I'd cook to heal and I'd cook to live. I learned through cooking that God didn't make me a failure and that life is much like perfecting a recipe. You start out with an idea, and if it fails, you keep trying until you've crafted a wonderful dish. And when you revisit that recipe years later, you improve it further by using the new things you've learned. To me, a recipe is never done; it's meant to be fiddled with, rewritten, just like life. As I grow and change, I hope to be better with each new day. I hope that I can always revisit old ways of doing things and incorporate the new lessons I've learned in the meantime. You have to hold on to good stuff and build upon it.

Stories of deep healing are woven throughout this book. These words represent how I've been polished through the years to shine the way I do today, all with an understanding that there's still polishing to be done, of course. There are recipes here too! They are simple and delicious; may each one remind you that you can *make it*. A symphony of living pours through these pages. Glorious triumphs, growing seasons, and finding wonderful things in pockets we thought were empty.

Here, the low and dark days mingle with such deep joy, all of it adding up to a beautiful slice of my life. If I can relay to your heart just a moment of my experience and point you toward Jesus and a love and a force and a God so sweet, then I'll have done my job. The power of the Holy Spirit, I've learned, is fierce and wonderful. We need to hear one another's stories, for they are powerful reminders that we can do this thing called life. Together. We are never alone. May I always be sweetly broken and filled with joy and hope, willing to share—sometimes even before I'm *ready* to share. May I always be vulnerable and real. My story isn't profound, my life no more worthy than any other. I've learned that simply getting out of my own way inevitably reveals a life that is precious, ordinary, and brilliant in extraordinary ways. All life is precious, and our stories need to be told.

Your life is, and always has been, a gift.

Everywhere You Go

Everywhere you go, there you are.

Often, I can't see what God is doing in a difficult moment because there I am in the midst of the thing, firmly in survival mode, trying to fix the problem at hand. Deep in the mire, I'm not focused on seeing how the hand of God is moving. There have been a few precious times in my life when I've known, in the moment, that God was in it with me, but usually it's only once I've sailed on from a particular moment that I realize the special work God was doing on my behalf.

I once owned a restaurant, a magical place called Minoela. But a lot went wrong, and Minoela was closed. It wasn't until I was picking up the pieces in the aftermath that I could begin to see my north. That out of that wreckage, my true calling was being developed and refined. That Minoela's closing, while difficult at the time, was actually beauty twofold, for I'd learn about myself *and* about the heart Jesus had for me.

My name is Danielle Kartes. I am a gal who loves people *through* food. Through food, I am able to work on television, write cookbooks and children's books, and teach how feeding people is to truly, selflessly love them. Let's get nitty-gritty about real food and real life! I am a wife and a mother. I believe there is sanctity in mothering the two beautiful boys I have (boy moms—*whew*! Am I right?). I've learned of the deep sorrows and guilt felt in a mother's heart, and I've seen the freedom Jesus brings to that journey. Being a wife has taught me how to get along with another person and that I'm not always right. I mean, I'm right ninety-nine percent of the time, but that one percent, oh boy, is it humbling! There is an intense love available in marriage when we allow our expectations to fall away as we both serve the Lord first, then each other. Oh, and my guy is funny; that's a huge help!

Welcome to these notes about life. Here are some stories to fill your empty cup. This is a safe place for real people.

I pride myself on a grandmotherly style of cooking that draws comforting circles around people. It's a style that favors long braises and inexpensive ingredients at the height of their season to make food that is humble and beautiful. The way I see it, that's how it's meant to be. I love food that is wholesome, crave-able, and begging for just another bite—food for laughter and healing.

This, though, was not my initial perspective. When I first began, I wanted only the best of the best ingredients and to dabble in the newest food trends. I was an all-around foodie, for lack of a better word, but in the worst way. I wouldn't uncover the real me until after Minoela closed. Early on, real me was always hangin' around, but I'd bullied her into believing she wasn't worth much, that she was sort of a goofy mess-up.

The truth, of course, is that the real me was bright, innovative, and beautiful. It just took some catastrophe, some time, and some dust to settle and then be wiped off for me to see it.

I was recently listening to a woman speak about pouring from an empty cup. Often, we feel beaten down, broken apart, as if, no matter what, we couldn't possibly continue. We are too empty, with nothing left to pour from ourselves. These feelings are very real. But the moments we choose to put one foot in front of the other are moments that turn into hours, hours to days, and pretty soon we've made it through the days, nights, months, and eventually through the difficult season. We thought we couldn't possibly give more, that the energy and resources simply weren't there.

But then, all of a sudden, we look in the rearview mirror to see the tiny miracle moments that got us through. Though initially unable to pick out the miracles while in the storm, afterward, we are able to see how we had been clinging all along to God's glorious life rafts. Look for the life rafts in the storm, if you can. The life rafts of friendship, of sun on our faces. The kind words from a stranger, the much-needed rest. The discovered bird's nest containing the tiny miracle-of-life eggs. The check that arrived in the mail just when it was needed most. The times we were finally able to sleep or when we found some reminder in nature that we were not forgotten, that the creator of the universe never left us. That the times that were the most difficult produced the most fruit. Those times, the ugly bits, were actually the times we learned the most. We were humbled, and they brought richness to our experience, gold to our minds. The gold is the new perspective, the newly found patience or grace we've uncovered by living a hard story.

I didn't know how watching my mother make big pots of soup for the homeless (though we had so little ourselves) as a little girl was going to shape how I viewed *giving* for the rest of my life. There is always something to give. I didn't know that selling candy suckers out of my backpack in junior high to earn money to buy nice school clothes would forge in me an entrepreneurial spirit that is fiery in the best way. I couldn't possibly have understood that struggling in my marriage and nearly divorcing my husband would set us up for a love so deeply at ease and curious and safe.

During my restaurant days, I'd fiddle and tinker with ingredients, getting fully comfortable with the process of cooking. I was getting a full life's education on living in my tiny restaurant's makeshift kitchen. While roasting potatoes and checking for the perfect caramelization, I was getting a crash course in patience and experience for a career I hadn't even imagined myself in yet. By watching butter brown, I learned patience in the kitchen. Through roasting vegetables in parchment, I learned how every season must be seized before it passes. That great-tasting food was slow and methodical, and in a month's time, the wild garlic would be gone until the following year. Once I knew how to coax glorious flavors from humble, bright, fresh food, I was compelled to share the details with anyone who would listen.

We should use what we've lived through to make a life we love. It's not about goals and lofty destinations. It's purely about taking the lessons pulled from ugly times and learning moments and trying to be a little bit better with the Lord's help today. I don't long to relive any specific time period from my past; there's no experience I wish I could freeze and redo. The nostalgia of my former days is nothing more than a sweet fragrance. The lessons learned are what I use to build upon in trying to live a better today. I don't and won't always succeed, and I know I'll journey through barren and broken seasons to balance out each season of harvest, but I won't forget what God has done for His glory in my life. I'll keep building. He has given me hope, He has given me joy, and He has given me a voice to share.

I get things wrong on the daily, but I do truly love each day, moment by moment, one foot in front of the other, just breathing in this life. I am always going to make salad dressings and fondly recall Minoela. I'll always remember packed summer evenings at the restaurant, selling special order after special order of roasted potatoes and garlic aioli. I am always going to think about my marriage and God's redemptive love when I eat strawberry shortcake.

I'll always remember peanut butter sandwiches on the plane ride to New York City, just to make sure the ends continued to meet. I'll never forget Rachael Ray grabbing my hands and sharing on national television about the days when she had to pick between toilet paper or potatoes at the grocer. I'll never forget dragging my wagon down First Avenue in Seattle, carting ingredients I would prep in a broken little kitchen corner to appear on the local news station. I'll never forget the first time I set foot on *The Kelly Clarkson Show* stage where Kelly and I made pot roast.

My life has been *defined* by pot roast—hope and pot roast, to be exact. Life is lived in the in-between, and its true glory is always revealed if we keep going, keep pushing, keep building. Glorious and joyful days come from using *where we've been* to enjoy life *in the moment.*

In my case, it took losing my restaurant to start really living, to figure out I wasn't this girl who lost herself in the process of living. Life doesn't go as we plan; ugly stuff happens. We are often told we've lost who we once were. I've come to find out that's not the case at all. We are simply living, really finding out what we are made of along the way. In these pages, you'll find out how all that happened. I figured out how strong and driven I could be in times of loss. I found out I'd always been me. There was nothing that could sweep me aside, hide me away, or make me truly unrecognizable to myself or our Heavenly Father. Sometimes it takes the hard times and the mess to reveal we are, and always have been, precious. We can lose our way and establish poor habits that muddy our sense of self, but in ten years of tender lessons, I have learned to hear this message from the Lord: *You were always there. You never left. You were never not you. Now walk with me awhile and uncover that girl again. She's not far.* And I want to share that lesson with you.

Every sunrise and each new day is a unique opportunity to begin again with ourselves and the Lord, fresh and free from the guilt and pain of the day before. Some days, the weight of our circumstances is crushing. And, boy, have I felt the crushing: in the air sucked from the courtroom as we filed for bankruptcy, when there wasn't enough money to buy food, when my car was repossessed in the middle of the night. These are the times when we keep going and continue breathing. We keep leaning on our Lord for strength, and pretty soon we've not only made it through the day but we are able to look behind and see the hand of God on every moment, in every detail, tenderizing our hearts and drawing us back to Him.

Recently, I found a pair of brass herons for sale online. They were *stunning*, and they'd look beautiful on my desktop. I discovered them during a time when, after a season of struggle, I realized my attitude had shifted. I was feeling the presence of the Lord in a new way. The seller had posted before and after photos of the herons. When she first acquired them, they were tired looking and tarnished. Tenderly, she cared for them, cleaning, polishing, and cleaning them again until they were bright and beautiful, a stunning light golden brass. Through her care, the true glory of these little birds had been revealed. Just as with these herons, God's glorious plan for our lives is designed for Him to take us from tarnished and dirty to bright and brilliant, making us new and revealing the beauty within. These birds are a constant reminder to me of what the powerful love of Jesus has done in my life. I look at these herons often, the smaller bird looking up and the larger bird bent lovingly toward the tiny one. The beauty of these birds had always been underneath; they just needed some tender loving care to reveal their polished glory.

As the small yet significant stories from my life during the times chronicled here unfold before you, I hope you can see the hand of God in your own story, polishing and wiping away every stain, caring for you. I hope you can truly feel that all along, no matter how life has turned out for you, that you, darling, were always there, just waiting for the polishing, for the refining. You are worth more than rubies, even in your darkest hours, with a story all your own that's worth being shared. You were always there.

Lemon Roasted Fingerling Potatoes with Garlic and Lemon Aioli

2 to 3 pounds assorted fingerling
　　potatoes

¼ cup olive oil

3 to 4 sprigs rosemary, leaves
　　removed from the stem

2 lemons, one sliced very thinly, one halved

Salt and pepper to taste

GARLIC AND LEMON AIOLI

1 cup mayonnaise

¼ cup finely grated parmesan cheese

Juice and zest of 1 lemon

1 small clove fresh garlic, finely
　　chopped and mashed into a paste

½ teaspoon cracked black pepper

Salt to taste

Preheat the oven to 350°F. Slice the potatoes in half lengthwise, and place them on a baking sheet lined with parchment paper. Drizzle with the olive oil and rosemary. Add the thin lemon slices to the pan. Squeeze the juice from the halved lemon over the entire pan of potatoes. Season generously with salt and pepper, and toss to coat the mixture evenly. Roast for 40 to 60 minutes.

Mix the aioli ingredients, and serve alongside the potatoes. Keeps for 3 to 4 days in the fridge.

My Noel, My Gift

Have you ever tasted a Minneola tangelo? It's the most wonderful and whimsical varietal of citrus. If you saw it in the produce section, it would look like an orange, only its peel is smoother and more vibrant in color. It's fragrant, tangy, and juicy, almost as if you are peeling a sweet tart and devouring it before you lose the juice to the kitchen sink or pavement. These tangelos are juicier than any other citrus fruit I've ever tasted. They're a hybrid wonder, a cross between a pomelo and a tangerine. I dream of this citrus! Minneolas just make you feel wonderful. These little "oranges" have carried through as an integral part of the branding for my business for years, ever since their magic was first revealed to me.

I discovered them in my early twenties when I was new to the world of food and loved everything about cooking. I'd try to find things I'd never tasted before. I tried all the lettuces at the grocery store with delight. "Have you ever tasted watercress?" I'd ask my friends. I'd wander through the produce section as a form of therapy. When I found the Minneola tangelo, I always thought it was pronounced min-oh-lah. I tucked that pronunciation into the back of my mind and dreamed of owning a tiny restaurant one day where we'd serve up dishes containing the kind of splendor I found in that fruit. In my restaurant, I'd serve food that people would line up for. It would be a place of respite. To eat at my place would feel like dining al fresco in Italy...even though I'd never been there.

As a child and through my teenage years, I had big dreams of owning a bistro with my sister. We'd talk of opening a little place we called Atlas. Atlas would serve food from around the world! I imagined it would be in the city. I'd write menus and dream up dishes I'd never even tasted. As I grew out of my teenage years and into true adulthood, I never shook this longing to work in and own a restaurant. I began working in restaurants and loved it. I loved the kitchen in particular, the dish pits and walk-in refrigerators. I thrilled at seeing speed racks with partially cooked vegetables and potatoes or hotel pans full of steaming soup rolled right into the fridge to cool per health department standards. It was exciting seeing bins of fries dropped into hot oil, hissing and sputtering, and then watching the cooks whip around and throw steaks and burgers on the flat top.

I could work the line, I'd think. I knew I could. These experiences only fueled my desire for a place of my own.

After I met my husband-to-be, Michael, and we married a year later, I thought we needed something to pour into together. We were tired, our relationship was in this delicate phase, and I thought it'd be amazing for us to open *my* dream together. I was mistaken but didn't know it. I was twenty-six; I knew everything. One of our close friends asked jokingly if we were trying to get a divorce. We'd laugh it off, and Mike was a good sport.

I began looking for spaces to rent and came upon Sixth and Fawcett in Tacoma, Washington. When we walked in, it was filthy. Food was stuck to the walls in the bare kitchen space, and the flooring was ugly and awful. Decoupage magazine pictures covered the bathroom walls, and the whole space was painted with at least forty-five different colors. I saw potential, but Mike saw heartache. I couldn't be swayed; we were doing this. We acquired the lease.

It took just four weeks to outfit the space and transform it into a functioning restaurant. We opened shortly after our first wedding anniversary. We had the smallest budget ever. How do you open a restaurant for $10,000 on a credit card and the meager bit of cash coming in? Very carefully!

I quit my job training makeup artists, and it was full speed ahead. Paying for it all was like a game of *Tetris* with a budget. I saw a beat-up van with a painting logo on the side and called the stenciled phone number. The gentleman that answered was quirky and rough. I told him I had $1,000 and needed 1,500 square feet painted. I told him I'd buy the paint and pay in cash. He agreed. They sprayed the interior of the restaurant a deeply calming olive green. That canvas calmed Mike's nerves a bit.

I took to the internet to build a kitchen, buying sinks for pennies from closed-up places and rescuing steel tables and shelving from rusting out in sellers' backyards. Elbow grease was my best friend. We needed refrigerators, and I had next to no budget, so I'd scan Craigslist daily. I struck backdoor deals and found an industrial two-door fridge for $600. The guy dropped it off and said, "Look, I get hired to haul these things to the dump, but this one's got at least a year or two left in it. It's yours, but don't tell a soul I'm sellin' it to you!" Sold!

In just four weeks, I had put together a dream. I got a liquor license in record time and used the bulk of my budget for tables and chairs. I bought and hung a wooden sign to tell the world that Minoela was open. Just before we opened, I learned that I'd been pronouncing the name of my beloved tangelo incorrectly. It was min-ee-oh-lah, rather than min-oh-lah as I had long imagined. So I fiddled with the spelling to sync it up with the pronunciation in my mind—there no rules in my brain!—and Minoela was born. We use the word *Noel* to represent Christmas, a time to give and receive gifts. Minoela, or my Noel, was my gift. That's the significance of the name for me. The name Minoela rolled off the tongue, and oh, she was so beautiful.

We opened and business began to build. I'd hire friends and

family to prep, serve, and cook, and that always went south. I was too harsh, too demanding. I quickly realized what an undertaking the restaurant business is. All the romance had a dark underbelly. The employee turnover was intense. Paying bills on time and trying to figure out which employees are stealing from you doesn't lend itself to a beautiful demeanor all the time. But the beautiful parts were *so* beautiful. They were more than I could hope for.

I began to employ chefs who would teach me how to cook. I thought I could cook when we opened, but I discovered that I had much to learn. Close to three years in that kitchen alongside talented chefs and cooks provided a hands-on education. Fresh herbs and farmers' market produce were king. Fresh pasta kissed by lemon zest and Dungeness crab—these were the foods that made my heart sing, and when I served my food to people, they would be overjoyed. This was a bit of foreshadowing for the career I'd pursue in the future.

There was the menu, and then there was the *secret* menu that lived in my brain: the sauces and dressings and salads that became daily specials. I'd get to work and begin whipping up all kinds of foods that I'd never tried before, and if they were a success, they were worked into the regular menu. Brie was a cornerstone ingredient at Minoela. We put that cheese, baked to gooey perfection, on sandwiches and savory platters of olives and tomatoes. We became a place where people came to celebrate and share intimate moments. The ambiance, the music (live on weekends), the food, the simplicity—it was all I ever imagined and more.

I had found my calling, my purpose. I was so important in my tiny world. All the while, however, I grew more and more distant from Mike.

Oh my, how God loved me so much as to allow my dreams to crack and crumble, and how patient He was with me as I cried myself to sleep over my failures. *At least I have Minoela*, I often thought. Mike and I were discussing the ideas of separation and divorce at the height of Minoela's success. I had this fallback; he had his job. The timing seemed right. We'd made it about three years into our marriage, and perhaps now we should just focus on ourselves. I had ideas of opening more locations, and Mike wanted nothing more than to never set foot in the restaurant again.

One evening, a dinner was sent back for having far too much garlic in the pesto. I thought there had to be some mistake! I couldn't get enough of that garlicky burn. I went to the cooler and tasted the pesto. It was wonderful. I asked the kitchen staff to taste. They nearly spit it out. "The garlic! Oh my gosh, it's barely edible! It tastes like chewing on raw garlic cloves!"

No, I thought, there was no way! I wanted more garlic. I was convinced they were all wrong. I was putting extra garlic in every-thing. I even questioned the potency of the fresh garlic I'd been buying and chewed a whole clove, only to discover I loved it. What was going on? The craving for raw garlic was intense.

I was pregnant.

How could this happen? Well, I knew exactly how it hap-pened, of course, but Mike and I were not exactly on the path to a happy family. We were discussing separate lives and how that would need to play out. Now the discussions quickly revolved around how we were going to make this work because this baby was on its way! Where we were headed for an ending, suddenly we were faced with a fresh start.

The garlic cravings evened out eventually, but I'll always remember chewing on cloves, thinking they were mild and sweet. To this day, I add fresh garlic to everything, and every so often, if the fragrance is just right, it reminds me of new beginnings.

Caramelized Brie and Tomatoes

PREP TIME: *5–8 minutes* • BAKE TIME: *7–9 minutes* • SERVES: *4*

1 (8-ounce) wheel Brie

1 cup cherry tomatoes, diced

2 to 3 sprigs, whole, fresh, woody herbs,
   such as lemon thyme or rosemary

1 clove fresh garlic, finely chopped

Splash of aged balsamic vinegar

Sea salt and black pepper to taste

Baguette or crackers for serving

Preheat the oven to 425°F. Gently slice the top rind off the Brie wheel. Top with the tomatoes, herbs, garlic, vinegar, and salt and pepper. Bake 7 to 9 minutes until the tomatoes blister and the Brie is melty and perfect for smearing on bread. Watch this closely; your tomatoes may burn, and your Brie may separate if kept in the oven too long. Serve with sliced baguette or crackers.

Please Love Me

"There's the door, girl." My mom took my hands and looked into my eyes. "It doesn't matter who's here or how much money we spent on this party. You've gotta be sure in your heart. And if not, I'll meet you 'round back, and we will be outta here."

I smiled big; there was nothing in my life I'd ever been more sure of. Marrying Mike was my greatest choice, the greatest blessing. I didn't have any idea at the time, of course, but we were going to the brink of divorce together, and we were going to come back from it better for each other. We were going to become better versions of ourselves.

Marriage is a sanctifying act. It asks us to be selfless. It teaches us not to give in to our own selfishness. I'd always bought into the lie that our spouses complete us, and if they didn't, then they must be doing this whole marriage thing terribly wrong. Oh, how little I knew. I was twenty-six and felt like an old maid. What I wouldn't give to go back and shake that girl who thought she was an old bride! That girl with so many ideas of how it all *should be*. Those silly ideas were embedded deeper in my value system than I gave them credit for. They would need to be unlearned for my marriage to thrive. How funny that society pressures us ladies into thinking that. But there I was, so young and filled with hope, ready to walk down the aisle and meet my best friend.

The way Mike treated me was like a fairy tale: dinners, plays, concerts, and laughter. We began this romance I'd never even come close to before in my life. His wit and charm won me over. He was so intelligent. I admired his convictions. There was just one huge, missing piece.

At the time, Mike didn't believe in God. We'd sit through dinners, and I'd cry into my food, begging Mike to just give Him a chance. I'd always ask, "What've you got to lose?" He'd always grin and say, "But *you* can! You can think anything you'd like. It doesn't change my love for you."

At one point in our relationship, though I was falling in love and our relationship was strong, I concluded that because Mike was someone who didn't share my belief in the Lord, it was okay to part ways. Mike didn't necessarily want kids and marriage, and I knew I did. We had a healthy conversation, and I told him we shouldn't keep this up, because pretty soon I'd be in too deep.

We wanted the best for each other, and our whirlwind romance would have to take a step back. We would really think about it, we decided.

A few days passed, and Michael came over to my house to visit. He had grown up with religion but didn't have a relationship with Jesus, and that's not something to force. It's something extremely personal, and I couldn't just keep shoving Jesus in front of him for me to feel better. He said to me that he wanted to know Jesus the way I did. He'd never experienced this kind of faith before. He wanted to get married and have children with me. He wanted a life with me. He chose me. I was so madly in love with him. He was, and still is, the most interesting, tenderhearted man I've ever known.

Well, that was all I needed! Hot damn, this was *it*! I had several friends tell me I was making a mistake. Very few times in my life, I've known with total certainty that I was exactly where I was supposed to be. And marrying Michael was one of those times.

A few months after the wedding though, the tensions began. Where was the fairy tale I was supposed to have? Where was the doting husband I'd fallen for? We were both selfish and awkward, and I was too embarrassed to ask anyone for help. There were no more dinners away, no more concerts, no more late-night talking sessions. The butterflies were gone. In their place was an emptiness I'd never known. *Is this how it's going to be?* I thought. *We just get married and immediately disconnect?*

Living together wasn't easy. We both had ways we wanted

things done. We were both convinced we were one hundred percent right all the time. There was no compromising, but there wasn't any grandiose moment that caused distance, just a series of moments that drew us away from each other. Early in our marriage, we weren't listening to each other, we weren't praying for each other, and I was lost and afraid of what was happening to me. I was traveling a lot at this time, working as a makeup artist, and I thought I should be home more. We'd find happiness if I wasn't on the road so much.

Let's open a restaurant! I thought. I legitimately believed that opening Minoela would save my marriage. And in a funny and very roundabout way, it actually did.

Honestly, I have avoided exploring the feelings from this period of my life again in order to write about it, but in feeling it, I've been able to recognize a healing I hadn't known had taken place. Sometimes we have to jump in, no hesitation, to understand that we can stand in the water. It's not too deep. We are sturdy and able to handle much more than we give ourselves credit for. I'm an avid avoider of big emotions. I mean, I'll cry every day as a form of communication, but that's natural for me. I know all too well how the quick release of a good cry sets up a new, joyful perspective. Some of us are naturally predisposed to joy, and some are not. But I truly believe that God can give the gift of joy to anyone at any point in their lives. Even now, begin asking Him, and I promise there will be a transformation in your heart. It may be slow going, but it's real.

Joy is a lovely companion. She is comforting in the midst of sorrow and doesn't beg for center stage. She is soft and true and unflashy. She is a deep well to draw from, and she sits comfortably alongside sadness and grief. God's gift to my heart has always been to be able to experience deep joy in the midst of every storm.

There are some rejections that cut deeply, to our innermost being. We think we shouldn't feel this way, that our guts shouldn't churn in agonizing loneliness even as we're surrounded by people. That we shouldn't be rife with anxiety as our marriages erode. My husband had rejected me. The rejection ran deep, and I'd never felt such an emptiness. I was desperate for him to love me. It felt like what I had to offer at the time wasn't good enough. And I hadn't allowed Mike to feel the very real emotions he was feeling at the time, so that he, in turn, internalized all of it. I felt sick all the time.

We got married, felt lost, and opened a juggernaut of a restaurant that drained our bank accounts and gave us a new, fresh level of stress that we'd both never experienced before. My whole goal was to give us something we could have together, and Minoela, so it seemed, was the ironic nail in the coffin. In hindsight, our problems were not that big early on. We could have gone to therapy, gone on vacation, or adopted a dog. But instead, I opened a restaurant. The fulfillment I was looking for in my marriage did not reach fruition with the restaurant. Instead of drawing us closer, it put up a fence between us. Oh, Minoela and this magical, extremely difficult slice in time for me. Up to that point in life, I hadn't felt so creatively alive. Every day was an opportunity to make beautiful food. There were roasted vegetables and fish in parchment, sauces and aioli, and fresh pastas. Some nights, we had a line out the door. The wine, the chocolate cake piled high with macaroon batter, the Brie!

I was receiving incredible fulfillment from cooking, learning, and those magical summer evenings filled with pasta and farmers' market vegetables. But all the while, Mike was working all night at his job and coming home to an empty house. We were unknowingly building separate lives. We kept this dark and painful secret. My emotional health was shot. But I could make it on my own, I thought. Mike could be free from this prison we'd created. Two years into Minoela, I was on fire, captain of the ship, and writing my own destiny! The money was pouring in! *This is my calling. I'm finally here!*

Without Mike. I thought, *I guess that's fine. We're both unhappy.* It was time to separate.

One night, I had closed up and let the staff go home. It was around midnight. I stayed behind, cleaning and setting up for the next day's service. I felt invincible. Nothing could touch me. I was twenty-eight years old and very tough. No one needed to walk me to my car. I locked the door and got into my car, which was parked right out front. I buckled and connected my cell phone to the charging cord.

Just then, a stranger opened the passenger-side door! I started yelling, "Get out of here!" My hands seemed to stop working suddenly. What was he *doing*? He climbed into the passenger seat as

I continued screaming for him to get out. *He buckled his seat belt!* I was in a full panic, and I screamed, loud and long. The man said nothing at first, then, just as he opened his mouth to speak, the light came on in the art gallery next door to my restaurant. A woman's silhouette moved behind the front window. Another light flipped on. Just then, a car pulled up behind me, headlights glaring. The man undid his seat belt, jumped out and into that car, and it sped away. The shop owner stepped outside, and I was beside myself, shaken and crying. The entire ordeal lasted just seconds but felt like hours.

When I told Mike what happened, it didn't get much of a reaction from him. This broke me. I knew at that point that our marriage was over. I let my expectations define who we were, and failure was all around me. My pride was intense. I had been holding on to this *me, me, me* model unknowingly. I thought separating would be the best choice for our hearts, and then we could find happiness alone and move on from each other.

The one thing I hadn't yet realized was that I am responsible for my own happiness, not Mike. Mike wasn't married to me simply to bring me the moon and stars and joy on a platter each day. My joy was God's business. And our marriage couldn't heal until I embraced this and we put each other above our own selfish desires. Trust me, Mike was no peach. It takes two to tango, as they say, and he surely wasn't bringing much besides anger and disappointment to the table either.

You might be feeling the same way about your own marriage.

The grief in a broken marriage is overwhelming. You might be leaning into divorce, or you might have taken the journey into divorce. There is no condemnation. Let me tell you, firsthand, that God is in the business of restoring funky, broken, nasty situations. He has a heart for the brokenhearted. He had a heart for me. And for Mike. He has a heart for you even if you walked a journey into divorce. He wants to heal you; he wants to bring you a new beginning. I'm humbled and grateful he helped Mike and I together. He had a heart for my crumbling empire, and He had a plan for the two of us *together*. He continues to gently speak to my heart, to prompt change that shows me my life is less and less about me, and in that, I find true contentment.

Even now, as I write this, recollecting aloud about Minoela to Mike in the other room, he yells back, "Say that Mike was worried because he could taste financial ruin like a sour ash on the wind after a forest fire." We both laugh at that silly but painfully truthful sentiment. We were absolutely in for financial ruin. And as it turns out, sometimes God delights in restoration after ruin.

Water Always Finds Its Level

It didn't break for us all at once. It took three years for our lines of communication to wear down, for Mike and me to turn everything into a fight. To love so wounded that just the slightest suggestion felt like deep criticism. Have you ever experienced a medical illness where you needed to draw blood work often during healing? The lab technician will draw from the same veins, even if they aren't fully healed from the last draw. And it stings. When you are wounded and not fully healed, everything hurts. How do you find a path to healing in a marriage that is hurt, mean, or broken?

I believe it happens in time. It happens in waves of forgiveness. It happened for me when I started working on myself. It happens by choosing it. The problems won't get fixed overnight.

And of course, they didn't begin overnight. We kept working at Minoela and growing further apart. I slowly started praying for my heart to change. I didn't say "God, change me!" and suddenly everything was better. I cried out to the Lord, broken and confused, and I said, "I don't know how to be better. I just know I don't want to be divorced."

We were two very selfish people learning how to live as one unit. Both of us were trying, and there were moments when it felt like we'd be okay after all, but ultimately neither of us was making the essential strides necessary to overcome our own stubbornness and embrace cooperation. When we finally came to the conclusion that we'd go our separate ways, I was relieved. Free to live my life, I thought. We had no plan, and we weren't in a rush. But shortly after we made this decision, things took a turn.

I found out we were having a baby. I told Mike. We were shocked. We knew right then that we were both very lost, but we had a child to think about now. I can't speak for Mike, but I know this was the beginning of my heart softening.

You may have experienced incredible challenges in your relationship or marriage. These wounds are deep and take lots of time and work to heal. And both sides have to genuinely desire it above all else. Are you a bad person if you've chosen divorce? No! You are not. You are a person, living and trying the very best you can.

I never want my story to sound as if *I've made it* or *I did the right thing*. This is simply the way Michael and I worked it out. It took time and prayer, and the Lord truly used our little baby,

Noah, to help us get there. He used that time in our lives to make us step back and marvel at the wonder it is to have a baby. The world was on fire for us, but this tiny miracle calmed so much. We needed a huge lightening up. Noah did just that. He brought levity and laughter and pure joy.

Being Noah's parents felt more normal for us than running a restaurant at the time. When we found out we were having a baby, all talk of separating and divorce stopped. We had to try. We were having a child. It was a choice we made together, as a couple and as individuals. We were going to keep our heads above water and try to make our marriage work. And God met us there. We gave Him all of us, and He began working in our hearts. We didn't know that the year to come would see us closing the restaurant or that our lives would change to the extent that we'd lose nearly everything. We just knew that we had a baby coming and we couldn't give up.

I had to rely on Mike during my pregnancy with Noah. He had to care for me in a completely different way. In his care for me, we started to heal. The restaurant closed, and with it went all my dreams, but I had a new life, and I could focus completely on my little family. When we eventually moved away from the area, I could breathe a little more. A new city, a new life. By then, Noah was just about to turn two, and I remember we didn't talk about our struggles as often. Before Noah, our problems were all we talked about. Now we talked about this kiddo and the joy he brought us, and in not focusing on ourselves, we began to come back together.

One evening at bedtime, Noah knocked a big glass of water off my nightstand. The water soaked my pillows. I love pillows! I tuck three or four in all around me each night. I was able to salvage one that only had a wet corner, and after I cleaned up, hit the light, and tucked in for sleep, I told Mike I wished I had my pillows. "Sleep won't come easy tonight," I told him.

Mike said, "Oh, I have an extra. Here you go, babe." I thanked him, reached for the pillow, and fell asleep. The next morning, I woke up, and Mike had already left for work. I went to make the bed up, and I noticed that Mike's side of the bed had no pillows. He had told me he had an extra, but actually he had given me his one and only pillow, then slept without one.

I sat on the bed, and tears filled my eyes. This small, seemingly insignificant gesture meant more to me than flowers or nights out. He had sacrificed his own comfort for me. And I knew we were healing. I made his favorite spaghetti for dinner that night. I made pasta and added olives and peppers. Mike loves spaghetti. I mean, he really loves it! These small things helped us to appreciate each other, to knock down our walls.

Today, Mike and I have been married for fourteen years. He is my bright spot. We were at dinner the other day with friends, and I was expressing concern about raising our boys. I doubt so often! What if I'm not providing what they need? What if things don't work out the way I hope for them to? Mike looked over at me and said, "Water always finds its level." What truth! In hindsight, that phrase describes our marriage. A sloshing bucket will quiet itself after it's been bumped or kicked. The water moves about in a torrent at first, but it always calms eventually. Our relationship isn't perfect, but I would choose no other. We chose each other in spite of our faults, and as a result, we've always found our level.

God renewed our fractured relationship by healing each of us, first individually and then as a couple. And we are not done. But we choose each other every day. There is no magical formula or quick fix, but I know that grace for each other is life-giving. Grace must have a place in your heart. The grace we receive from Jesus is the only formula I know for success in marriage. Praying for your spouse and asking them for prayer. When Mike prays for me, I feel the presence of the Holy Spirit.

One profound lesson Mike taught me is that we can't take back ugly words once they've left our mouths, but we can always seek forgiveness for saying unkind things. You can seek forgiveness, but the words linger. In disagreements, a bit of restraint can save you from having to apologize at all. I used to fight so ugly. It's all I ever knew. I grew up finding the ugliest things I could say to win. But there can be no winning in a fight with your spouse. When winning the fight is the goal rather than real communication, you say awful things! During a particularly nasty fight, Mike asked me, "Do you love me?"

I immediately said no.

He asked again. "Put your anger aside. Do you love me?"

I reluctantly said, "Yes." I did love him.

He said something then that I'll never forget. He said, "If you love me, you can't say these things. You can never say these hateful things to someone you love."

It changed how I speak to him, how I speak in anger altogether. Saying bitter things, even if we think they are justified, plants seeds of bitterness in our hearts. Here we are, fourteen years later, and we are more in love because we understand now that we are each responsible for ourselves.

The notion that your spouse must complete you and make you happy is false. Of course, marriage isn't an invitation or a permission slip for being mistreated. Communication is of utmost importance, and fair arguments about how you are feeling are key, but most of all, prayer works. Prayer sets the stage for contentment and a desire to do kind things for your spouse. Prayer opens the doorway to heaven inside your relationship, and it puts you second and God first. Love is selfless, and in that selflessness lies fulfillment. The self-care movement would have you cutting off everything that you see no need for, but let me tell you, there is no more powerful love than to lay personal needs aside for another. These are the things that healed Mike's and my marriage. These are the paths we chose to make a gift, given to each other, of our marriage.

I also think I stopped taking everything so seriously. We started laughing again. We are both weird and funny, and I loved that about us. We gave life to the good stuff, not the bad. I love Mike more today than I ever have. I love everything about him. That doesn't mean we don't fight; it just means that we know the grass isn't greener and compromise is sexy.

We see the gifts in our lives because we chose our marriage. Our kids, our business, our partnership—it's all blessed, and I know it's because we stayed. Divorce isn't always the answer for healing. In our case, it wasn't, and I hope this helps you to pray for that bratty partner driving you wild right now. God can fix it. He fixed us.

Seven Pounds, Eleven Ounces

The hospital lights were glaring. The nurse fiddled with discharge paperwork on her computer.

"I'm sorry, but you may be losing the baby," she said. "People have miscarriages all the time. Heck, I've had three! I also have healthy kids. It's perfectly natural."

This couldn't be happening. My mind spun. My chest was tight, and I couldn't speak. My eyes brimmed with tears.

"You'll be just fine. Don't cry. I promise it'll be okay."

I'd never heard anyone speak so cavalierly about a baby. This was not happening. These people were wrong. This nurse was a horrible person! I wanted to get out of there! Her well-intentioned yet insensitive comments lit a fire in my heart. I couldn't lose this baby. This baby still had a heartbeat.

I was about nine or ten weeks along, and I had gone to the emergency room for bleeding. They let me know I was likely losing the baby. I felt hollow. But as we pulled into our driveway, I saw a rainbow above my home, and I knew in my heart that the baby would make it. I spent the afternoon calling doctors. No one would see me until after twelve weeks, or I'd need a referral to a specialist. I called a doctor's office, crying. Most receptionists were very kind and explained that it's best practice to see patients after twelve weeks. One receptionist, though, heard me out. I needed to see a doctor who could help me, and she was the only one who put me on hold and came back to say they could fit me in the next day. "We will need a referral, and we can get that from your primary care." She could tell I was distressed. "Don't cry, sweetie," she said. "What you are going through is very difficult. We will see you tomorrow."

The doctor was kind and had a matter-of-fact nature. I was relieved to hear that the baby's heartbeat was strong.

"The ER isn't trained for things like this. I think you've got an early case of preeclampsia."

My blood pressure was through the roof. He informed me that his office didn't normally handle cases of preeclampsia this soon. "But," he said, "we will get you on medicine and watch you very closely. You are now a porcelain doll, to be put on a shelf."

No more long days in the kitchen. No more whimsical recipe testing and secret menus. Bed rest was my new normal. Mike stepped in to care for me in ways he never had before. He would put in ten to twelve hours at work, then do the shopping for the restaurant and head to Minoela while I was home in bed, often serving as manager for the dinner shift.

I had three standing doctor appointments per week. I only showered once or twice a week. No stress, no lifting, no strenuous activity of any kind. Definitely no running a restaurant. Mike continued managing Minoela in addition to his regular job. I can't speak for him, but I believe this was the beginning of the softening of his heart. The restaurant slowly stopped having wildly busy nights. The lines disappeared, and the seats were empty. During those seven months, many employees quit, and the money dried up.

I wasn't there to oversee the business like I had been before. I wasn't cooking anymore. My presence at Minoela had proven invaluable, but now I was growing a baby and watching our bank accounts dwindle to whispers.

We were having a darling boy. I had a dream that I was standing in the middle of Minoela in the evening. I asked a woman if she'd met my son, Noah. Noah was his name; I was sure of it. A tiny life in me that came from two lost people just trying to find their way.

On the first morning of my thirty-seventh week, my water broke and labor began. At 5:20 a.m. the following day, the baby came. When they put him on my chest, I cried. We'd made it! This pudgy, squishy child in my arms had survived. Welcome home, darling boy!

All of a sudden, I didn't care so much about Minoela. All I could think about was Noah. My needs? Out the window in the best possible way. I was mesmerized.

Minoela closed its doors for good just four days after Noah was born. We put an ad out for a going-out-of-business sale. At one point in my life, I'd have bet the farm I was born to be a restaurateur. Now, here I was closing the business of my dreams, selling everything inside that wasn't nailed down at a sidewalk sale spearheaded by Mike.

I sat at home holding Noah, just days old. My phone rang. "It's all gone, babe. They came in swarms," Mike said. Three years of work gone in an afternoon. "They bought the paper towels and toilet paper. They bought the mop bucket! I've got $11,000 in my pocket. I'll grab a burger for you and head to the bank." Mike dropped the building keys through the mail slot and drove away for the last time. And $11,000 was exactly what we owed in back excise taxes.

I felt numb, but I also felt massive relief. No more heartache. No more payroll, rent, and overhead stresses. Just the three of us now.

Over the next couple of years, we'd lose most everything except each other. Mike came home that day after the sidewalk sale with loads of pound cakes, half gallons of cream, berries, and the rest of the wine inventory, along with other odds and ends. We ate pound cake, cream, and berries for dinner all that summer. We'd lie on our bed with the precious baby between us, marveling at what a wonderful thing he was, softening toward each other. Eating cake. We began to laugh again. The wreckage still smoldered, but we were leaning into one another because we had Noah. Nothing else mattered.

In recalling Minoela's opening day, I'm struck by the vividness of the memory: music playing, tables set and ready to receive guests. God spoke to my heart: *I'll take care of you through this place.* After its failure, I questioned God and reminded Him of His promises. We had nothing. *God, you promised to care for me!*

And He most certainly was. Even in our most sorrowful times, I enjoyed the gift of never feeling abandoned or forsaken by the Lord. I never felt that He wasn't there. At times, he was quiet, but I understood I needed to match His quietness to hear Him. I needed to mute my needs and complaints to feel His presence in our lives.

The year that followed our business failure was the year Mike and I fell in love again. I went back to work full-time when Noah was just eight weeks old. I was doing makeup and trying hard to pretend the last three years hadn't happened the way they did. Mike would work from 2:00 a.m. till about noon, then drive home, meeting me along the way in a parking lot where we'd trade the baby and car seat and I'd continue on to work.

I started noticing things about Mike, again *and* for the first time. He was a sweet friend, patient, fair, and kind. He was sharp in wit, dryly comic, and the most loving father. Watching him with Noah opened up parts of him I knew even he didn't know were there. I started understanding that he didn't complete me; that wasn't his job. He was not responsible for making me happy or authoring my dreams. I began learning that marriage gets really good when you decide that your spouse isn't responsible for you. They *add* to your life. I began forgiving him for how he treated me early on. So much pressure went out the door when I started allowing him to be who God created him to be. We had a beautiful life together, and I just started seeing it. Mike is my friend, my business partner, a confidant, and a man to weather the storms with. He's my treasure-hunting companion forever.

I learned then that I needed to stop longing for the butterflies of our dating days because God was ready to build a fire between us if only we'd allow Him to. I'm Team Fire; you can keep every cutesy butterfly! This man is my fire! He brings so much life to my world and makes me laugh. He's smarter than I could ever dream of being. I can only hope to one day fully understand the art in his eyes.

Pray for your partner. War for them. Lift them up even when it's painful. I started choosing Mike and sacrificing for Mike, and he began the same for me. This took years, of course. The damage to our marriage didn't happen overnight, and the healing, in turn, took its time. And the work doesn't stop; we still have to fight to work through things together. We go deep, and if it's ugly, it needs to come to the surface so that we can pray through it as a team.

The financial fallout from closing Minoela had left us with debt. We worked hard every month to pay it back, but it proved insurmountable in the end. About a year and some change past the closing of Minoela, we filed for bankruptcy.

It felt heavy in that courtroom. My body ached from the burden of picking up the pieces in the wake of shutting Minoela's doors, and our case was approved. We left the city where we had been living and moved to a little apartment an hour away so that Mike could be closer to work.

We had no friends, no community. Just each other. And our boy. The next five healing years would produce more fruit than I could ever have imagined. It became a time of planting for a harvest I knew nothing about. We worked hard to make ends meet. I worked as a makeup artist, and Mike delivered bread. It was a very simple time, full of reconciliation and trusting the Lord. God began to breathe a new vision into our hearts.

After trauma has entered the building, it's difficult to dream again. When Noah was just six months old, I thought I'd write down the recipes from Minoela so I wouldn't lose them. I vowed to never cook again—cooking had cost me everything.

But I've heard it said in our greatest weakness lies our greatest strength. My cooking days were far from over, and this was just the beginning.

Honey Butter Biscuit Strawberry Shortcake

PREP TIME: *15 minutes* • INACTIVE TIME: *30 minutes* • BAKE TIME: *15–20 minutes* •

YIELD: *Roughly 12 biscuits*

HONEY BUTTER BISCUITS

2¼ cups all-purpose flour,
   plus more for dusting

2 tablespoons baking powder

1 teaspoon salt

½ cup cold butter, diced into cubes
   and smooshed into flat discs

1 cup heavy whipping cream

¼ cup honey, plus more for drizzling

2 to 3 tablespoons melted butter

STRAWBERRIES

3 to 4 cups fresh strawberries

½ cup brown sugar

2 tablespoons freshly
   squeezed lemon juice

Pinch of salt

CRÈME FRAÎCHE WHIPPED CREAM

1 cup crème fraîche

1 cup heavy whipping cream

½ cup confectioners' sugar

1 teaspoon vanilla extract

Add the flour, baking powder, salt, and butter to the bowl of a food processor, and pulse. Whisk the cream and honey together in another bowl. Slowly add the honeyed cream to the flour mixture, and pulse a few times until the mix comes together to form a shaggy dough. Dump the contents out onto a floured surface, and form into a 10-by-6-inch rectangle. Fold the rectangle in half, and place in the fridge to rest for at least 30 minutes.

Preheat the oven to 400°F. Remove the rested dough from the fridge, roll out into another 10-by-6-inch rectangle, and fold over on itself. Roll into a 10-by-6-inch rectangle a third and final time. Cut the dough into 8 to 10 squares using a serrated bread knife, and arrange on a baking sheet lined with parchment paper. Brush the tops of the biscuits with melted butter and a drizzle of honey before baking. Bake for 15 to 20 minutes, until puffed and golden.

Wash and slice the berries in half, then put them in a bowl and gently fold in the sugar and lemon juice. Allow to stand at room temperature for at least 30 minutes so the berries can make a nice syrup with their own juices.

Combine the crème fraîche, cream, sugar, and vanilla, then whip on high, just until soft peaks form.

Assemble individual shortcakes by topping biscuits with strawberries and crème fraîche whipped cream.

Fig Syrup

The most delicious and beautiful foods to ever come from my hands and heart are unplanned. They are spontaneous and show up when I least expect them. Last night, I needed to just spend some time with the Lord. A lot of times, if I feel distant from God, it's because I'm just not spending time in His presence. Sometimes, all the distractions need to fall away, and I need to stay focused on who He says I am.

So when my boys fall asleep, I'll go into my kitchen. All is quiet, and I can spend time with the Lord and cook. I'll cook jams or jellies. I'll boil eggs or bake bread. The tasks late at night have no deadline. They need not be photographed. They are simply a creative expression in steps where I can talk with Jesus. On one particular evening, I remembered I had some pretty special figs in the refrigerator. When all was quiet and the last of the sun had sunk below the tree line, I pulled from the fridge these beautiful, soft figs from our friend's tree. I'd let them sit in the fridge a day too long, and by this time, if I didn't do something with them, they'd spoil. I love the figs, called Desert Kings, that grow here in the western Washington area where I live. They have bright-green skin and deep-rose-colored flesh. They are fruitier than most figs, and they just drip with delicious, sweet juice when you tear them apart. They taste especially wonderful with Brie and olive oil toast and salty, delicate slices of prosciutto. I decided I needed to pray, and I cooked.

I love to make fig jam each year. I boil the glorious figs with sugar and lemon, and they always turn into a thick and delicious brown jam to accompany cheese. I placed the figs into an enamel-covered saucepan. The white interior looked so pretty against the green figs. As I turned on the heat, a bright, beautiful syrup appeared, as it always does when I make fig jam. I normally linger, really enjoying watching the sweet pink syrup swirl about the pan as it fades to a tan color and then begins to thicken into the jam I'm used to. But in that moment, I decided to just spoon that pretty syrup into a jar and see what would happen. What happened was glorious and delicate fig syrup. I've never tasted anything quite like it: floral and tart, with these crunchy little seeds. It was a delight! I usually cook the figs into a jam for cheese plates and Newton-style cookies. But this time, stopping at this syrup phase turned out incredibly well! The syrup kept its delicate color and flavor.

Sometimes, we plan it all out—the goals, the Instagram posts, our next moves, the family activities, and career five-year trajectories. I know I plan and strive and try and push. But sometimes the Lord is quietly whispering to our hearts to come away with Him and see what happens. He desires to fulfill His purpose in our lives for His glory. Sometimes you'll get beautiful and delicate syrup, better than any jam you've ever planned, if only you'll listen to His heart. I think we are always the most ministered to in the quiet, everyday moments with Jesus.

It might sound silly that this time He used figs to reveal His heart to me, but I am in awe that He relentlessly pursues our hearts in the tenderest way. I believe that He has a word for you where you least expect it if you just follow His lead. His yoke is easy, His burden light. Allow Him to heal whatever hurts in your life. Spend some time *unplanning* right now.

I imagine tiny grandmothers eating fig syrup in Italy or Greece, taking small sips of whatever liqueur is in the cabinet. When you feel far from home or unstable in this life, remember who God says you are. You are precious and loved and important to Him. Spend time quietly anticipating His heart for your life. See what delicate syrup He has waiting for you if you slow down with Him, give your plans to Him. I hope you can get some figs and a few quiet moments to try this recipe because this syrup is heaven.

Fig Syrup and Jam

PREP TIME: *10 minutes* • COOK TIME: *40–50 minutes* • YIELD: *Roughly 12 ounces syrup and 12 ounces jam*

1½ pounds fresh figs

1 to 2 cups sugar (depends on the sweetness in your fruit)

Juice of two lemons

Combine the ingredients in a saucepan, and cook over medium heat until syrupy and bubbling, maybe 5 to 10 minutes. Spoon off the fragrant syrup. Store in mason jars with lids for up to 14 days. Continue cooking the pulp to make jam, roughly 35 to 40 minutes. Be careful to watch for sticking once you've removed the syrup.

A Pocket Full of Pretzels

"Great talk, Danielle! We appreciate you, and you're doing a great job!"

I slurped the latte that my boss had bought for me and waved goodbye to her as I left the coffee stand and headed back to the Laura Mercier makeup counter where I worked. *You are doing a great job, Danielle.* I hadn't heard that in a long time. In fact, it was rare for me to be praised in any sort of work setting, but honestly, I didn't always do a great job. And a few months before, my life had nearly fallen apart because of it.

I'd always been fired from my jobs. A combination of insecurity, poor time management, and just plain lack of skill always led, after a couple of shaky years, to inevitable unemployment. It's comical now to think about how *often* I was let go! My dad used to say that every great man (or woman, in my case) was fired at some point. I clung to that proclamation. I'd make the walk of shame out to the parking lot, personal effects in hand, and blame whoever it was this time who couldn't handle me. I'd think to myself, *Man, I'm better off! They can't handle my greatness!* The truth is, I couldn't handle my greatness. Ouch. Reality is rough sometimes.

I needed training. I needed healing. I needed grace for myself and others...and it was coming.

At the age of twenty-nine, I was starting over again, essentially fired from my own business. Sort of like when Steve Jobs was removed from Apple that one time. I mean *sort of* only because instead of the board removing the genius, in my case it was more like the landlord, wanting her money and not receiving it, deciding to shut us down. My actions, though well-intentioned, had chipped away at the foundation of the business my husband I had built together and, simultaneously, at our marriage.

Minoela was a beautiful restaurant, *our* restaurant. We opened on a shoestring budget, thrifted our equipment, and brought our scrappy attitudes to every detail. I'd pieced together the kitchen off Craigslist, and I poured my heart and soul into that tiny space on the corner of Sixth and Fawcett Avenue in Tacoma. I learned how to make fresh pasta and hot sandwiches as big as your face and salad dressings from scratch that would make customers cry. We'd dry the pasta from the rungs of the dish racks and make roasted vegetables in these buttery pouches of parchment paper.

The regular menu was great, but the specials were magnificent. Potatoes dripping in olive oil, garlic, and fresh herbs served alongside homemade parmesan aioli. Crisp salads and heirloom tomatoes towering between slices of fresh mozzarella and chive pesto.

During our prime, the food was incredible, and everyone in town knew it. There was a line out the door most nights. People came in to have a slice of chocolate cake topped with gooey, buttery macaroons or a French press coffee and the same warm cake drizzled in double heavy cream, topped with blueberries. August was always my favorite month. The farmers' markets were packed with beautiful produce, and I'd stop in to buy all the veggies and make gorgeous food back at Minoela. I learned that a talented cook lived inside me. I'd only seen snippets of her before in my life. I was creative and did things differently. I learned new techniques from each chef I was lucky enough to employ.

Now, standing at that makeup counter in the mall, I felt so far from who I had been not that long ago, making pasta and big pots of puttanesca sauce loaded with garlic, chilies, kalamata olives, and anchovies. Now, here I was, a failed restaurateur and once-again makeup artist, just as I had been in my early twenties, back before the grand adventure of Minoela. My marriage was recovering from incredible stress. I had a twelve-week-old son. I stood sipping the dregs of my coffee, letting the reality of my situation sink in at the worst possible time. I would smile as authentically as possible and invite shopping passersby over to the counter for a lesson in the latest beauty trends. I would sell as much makeup as possible, remaining as upbeat I could. But tears would sometimes well in my eyes. I thought, *Isn't it funny? It's funny that just a few months ago, I was running my own restaurant!*

And now things had changed. I was saying goodbye to ugly things. We all have some ugliness that needs to be drawn out of us. The journey of ridding myself of thoughts and behaviors I'd once believed were necessary to live "a great life" was just beginning.

Earlier that morning, I had prepared to head to work. We didn't have much food in the house, and it was a few days till payday. I needed to make sure the boys ate the few eggs we had left along with the string cheese, making sure there would be one egg left for me to eat upon returning home. There wasn't enough food for me to bring something to work with me, so I had filled a plastic freezer bag with snacking pretzels and tossed it into my purse. I figured the pretzels were just enough to munch on and get me through the workday, then I'd eat the last egg that evening.

While at work, I'd withdraw a pretzel or two from the tiny pouch snugly tucked into the pocket of my brush belt, and eat them. Eating on the sales floor wasn't exactly smiled upon by the powers that be. My boss would sporadically come by during my shift, and as soon as the coast was clear again, I'd tuck my hand into the pouch and snag a bite.

Well before the end of the workday, the pretzels were gone. And this overwhelmed me. That tiny bag of pretzels seemed somehow a representation of my life in that moment. I took a break and walked away from the makeup counter feeling helpless, my hopes dashed. Who was I? How was I ever going to get out of the mess I'd made of my life? I was embarrassed. I was barely providing for my son, selling lipstick and trying to silently pick up the pieces, talking to none of my colleagues about what I was going through. None of them knew I'd lost all our money when Minoela went under. Or that I'd made a mess of my marriage.

On my way to the restroom, eyes blurred with tears, I ended up in the ladies' department. I was a puddle. I had been carrying the weight of the world on my shoulders, trying to keep it all together. But something about the beautiful department store dresses and gowns struck me, and I stopped. A feeling of hope washed over me. *It won't be this hard forever*, I thought. *You will have food in your cupboards again, to overflow. God created you for a purpose.* I felt a few of the dresses, my hands gently caressing the fabric. And just like that, God made this profound promise to my heart. *Someday, you'll need a dress like this. Where you are going, you'll need it.* Tears gently began to fall from my eyes, and there was a lump in the back of my throat. God was making me a promise that I wouldn't always struggle to enjoy life or merely make it through. My worth extended beyond any title or job that I held.

That empty pocket of pretzels had delivered me into a pivotal moment, the moment I let the idea of failure fall from my mind with each tear. I was in agreement with the Lord for the first time in a long time. I had failed, but I wasn't a failure. I had messed up, but I was not a mess-up. I was and am a child of God, daughter of the King, made for more, made to rise above difficult circumstances.

Things seemed bleak and impossible, but where I was headed, I'd need a beautiful, regal dress.

It seems obvious in hindsight, but it had been a long time coming. The healing process had begun. The process of putting back together a very broken woman, a woman who had lived most of her adult life measuring her worth based on her success. God knows and remembers every tear. He keeps a record of each one, he knows the pain they represent, and no tear is ever wasted. God uses our brokenness for His glory in our lives.

I think back now on that moment, and I realize that those dresses saved me. I needed to see myself as a woman who deserved a beautiful gown. Those gowns represented a way of thinking about myself. We all deserve to view ourselves clothed in something magnificent and lovely. Not shame, not hardship. Bad things happen, but they're not who we are. We are meant for more. We are more than the sum of the crappy situations we endure, even when they're caused by our own doing.

I'd spend the next five years at the makeup counter with Laura Mercier, healing and turning the life I once believed to be all I ever wanted into the stepping-stones necessary to love who I was. In the years to come, I would discover that I was a writer, that I was a good mom, that I had a brilliant marriage. That I had gifts I had not known about tucked away inside me. I would find that I still loved to cook, and I would start a business called Rustic Joyful Food. I'd begin to teach women how to love their lives today, right where they are, even when it's hard. I'd turn my recipes scribbled on servers' notepads I had tucked away in boxes into a cookbook. And I'd start a career I'd never planned for but had unknowingly been preparing for. Who knew that makeup sales would heal my heart? But they did. I'd spend the next five years growing, writing, and dreaming. I'd learn to mother, terribly on some days and saintly on others. I learned that arriving to work on time and restraint in speaking my mind about *every single terrible customer* could be a training ground for my calling in life.

I often hear people say they don't know who they are anymore, that they are perhaps a shadow of who they've been. The truth is we never really lose ourselves. I believe we are in there always, our truest selves, during the hardest times especially. The real "us" never stops learning, growing, and becoming better.

The metaphor of the refiner's fire explains it best. There is a process to making many precious metals. The refiner or metalsmith must heat the dross to a certain temperature to remove impurities and reveal the silver or gold. When we face affliction and trials, I believe it can be used as a refining process in our lives. The silver was always there—it merely required the fire's purification to become precious. The silver was always there. You were always there. Never lost. Life's trials were simply refining you, transforming that raw hurt into passion for life.

It's been several years now since I left the makeup world for good. But I recently called my old boss at Laura Mercier to thank her for believing in me and putting up with me during my "ugly" years. The time I spent as her employee gave way to the life I have today. She was kind to me, and she never fired me; she displayed total grace. I learned to be a proper employee from her, and I learned something about being a better employer too. I learned to forgive myself at Laura. I will always treasure that time in my life.

And I will always know that that pocket full of pretzels was a catalyst for me to believe in the woman I was and to know that God doesn't make junk. God graced you with flaws, each with a designated purpose, each with an aim to help you grow. He has gifted you with every talent to fulfill His glory in your life. When we start living in purpose instead of going through the motions, we begin to heal, and it's a little bit easier to get through the day. The anxiety gets a little less loud, and the fear becomes a little softer. There is glory in the everyday. I see now that every day, no matter how big the trial or mundane the task, I am exactly where I'm supposed to be. And joy can live amid sorrow.

I'm grateful for pretzels and lipstick and tears. Don't wish away the training years. These are the years the diamonds are mined.

Hope and Pot Roast

"You have a baby?"

"Yes, he's six months old! He's my whole world." I stepped into the elevator with one of my coworkers after a long day, dressed in all black and feet aching.

"I am just surprised," she said. "Normally, people with kids talk about them nonstop." She rolled her eyes.

I replied, "Yes, well, I don't know. I'm new at being a mom, and I do have a beautiful baby boy named Noah. He keeps me very busy."

"Yeah, I bet," she said. "Well, I love that you don't just talk about him nonstop." That comment stung.

I didn't have much in common at this point with anyone I

worked with. It was no fault of their own. How could I possibly tell these girls what I was going through? They weren't married and loved to chat at the counter about dating and parties and shopping on their breaks; they were twentysomethings, fun and frilly, as they should be.

I doubt they'd have understood had I told them what I was going through. None of them had kids. They didn't have the same worries. The truth was that I was sad. I was learning how to cope and find joy amid my sadness.

Mike was working swing shifts, leaving somewhere between 1:00 and 3:00 a.m. every day to deliver bread. I'd start my shifts at noon. I'd work for around six hours, then head home. Because of Mike's schedule, I'd be up all night with Noah if he was restless. He wasn't a good sleeper. (This is when every mama from here to the moon lets out a sigh because she knows how tough it is to be up all night with the baby and then go to work the next day.)

Mike was such a good father. He cared for Noah so tenderly. He just needed to get in bed around 7:00 p.m. to be up at 2:00 a.m. I'd hold Noah most of the night so he and Mike could sleep, then I'd lay him in his crib once Mike was off to work. If all went well, then I could get some rest.

As time went on, I settled into loving work as a makeup artist again. I was letting go of a lot of things I'd held on to tightly for so long. Some of the women I thought I'd never have much in common with would become my dearest friends over the next five years. They were my champions. The relationships I built then have lasted to this day.

But at first, I felt so lost among these women, and it took a while for me to let some of them in. But I learned that every woman there would fiercely support my dreams and understand my struggle. Each of these women was just trying to make it through, like me. They just had their own set of struggles.

As the years went on, my sadness faded, and I realized I was always me. I was never the lost soul I had thought I was. I was okay—more than okay! I was brilliantly and wonderfully made.

During this time, a routine was set, and that felt good. In order for Mike and me both to work, we needed to meet on the road between our respective workplaces and trade off Noah. While Mike was finishing his day, I'd just be getting started. We'd meet each other in a Starbucks parking lot. Michael would quietly open the back passenger-side door and unhook Noah's car seat, then lift the whole thing, along with the sleeping toddler, and move the child's seat to his car.

We'd just started the process in figuring out how to file for bankruptcy. My life was a shadow of what I'd always hoped for.

But the truth was that in the midst of all this pain, Noah was our joy. He was pure happiness with pudgy cheeks and a toothy grin. He was determined, and he smelled like angels singing. I'd hold him each day after work, and we'd just stare into each other's eyes. He was this tiny hope. Each time I felt like the world was on fire, he reminded me that it was going to be okay. I'd whisper to him as he fell asleep in my arms each night. "You are a good leader. You are gifted. You are strong. You are perfectly and wonderfully made. God doesn't make mistakes. You are funny. You are handsome. You are meant to be the head and not the tail. You are the lender and not the borrower." I was speaking to my own heart too.

Later that year, sitting in a bankruptcy attorney's office, we learned that we would have to pay $1,200 to file, stop the harassing calls, and close a chapter of our lives that was such a mess. I think this was the first time I ugly cried in front of a stranger. The room felt small, and I could barely breathe. I told him I was sorry. I felt sick to my stomach. We just couldn't pay anyone back after closing Minoela. I cried and told him how I would go to the ATM in the middle of the night on Michael's paydays to pull grocery money out before the bill money was withdrawn, just to get through the next few days. Within hours of his paycheck hitting, our account would be in the red, and we'd have nothing for another week.

This cycle had gone on for almost a year before we searched for help and solemnly decided that if we could swing it, we'd have to file for bankruptcy. It took us four months to get the $1,200 together. We filed, sat in court, and told the judge. I fought back tears at the embarrassment of failing.

When it was our turn to speak, the judge asked if I had anything valuable. "You know, a Tiffany lamp, a secret inheritance. Anything of value you've been keeping hold of we should know about?"

I had a tiny box of silver coins. I said, "I've got this small box of silver coins, worth a few hundred bucks." He smiled and said, "Well, you can keep 'em."

Thanks, I guess? I'd never been so upset and so relieved. It was over. Just as quickly as it started, it was over. Because of the filing, we were losing our home and cars. We sold our condo and had to be out of there quickly. When my family came to help us move, I didn't even have moving boxes. We just put everything we owned into black garbage bags and threw it into the back of the moving truck. My brother-in-law joked that the move felt illegal.

Losing it all and throwing what we had in the back of a truck, then getting the heck outta Dodge. We moved an hour north to Issaquah, Washington, where we rented a little apartment and started over. Issaquah didn't feel like home for a really long time. Nothing did. But the stresses of life felt very few compared to the year we had just gone through.

I think Issaquah will always be special to me. It was a quiet time in our marriage. We had a toddler and a new rhythm. We rented a little garden plot in our apartment complex, and in that garden, there came quiet purpose. A calm after the storm. Mike went to work, then I went to work, and we were terribly happy. We didn't have an abundance of money, but we sure had an abundance of love. It sounds so silly, but I loved that little apartment. We'd invite friends over and eat sitting on the floor and the couch. We hosted parties, and I created the most beautiful food in that place. I learned that a great kitchen is never needed to create amazing food. I fostered a dream in Issaquah. We mended a marriage there.

We opened our new business, Rustic Joyful Food, in that apartment. We had another baby there.

Slowly but surely, tiny steps toward really understanding Rustic Joyful Food took place. What was our goal with this little food and photography company we had formed? What was my message? How could I ever tell people about hope *and* pot roast? The two seemed so separate at the time. I wanted to teach people how to cook, and I also wanted to teach people that there is always hope; I just didn't know how to marry the two. I learned that you *just do*. You just share. You keep sharing that hope and pot roast go hand in hand. I learned that people needed to know that joy and sorrow could live with one another. I had this deep need to be transparent in my struggles with the purpose of helping other women. I also wanted to share what I'd learned about cooking from my restaurant. There were so many methods for making pasta, for braising meat. I needed people to learn how to use up the food they had. It was this wild and exciting time, looking back. During those years, it didn't feel wild or exciting. It felt like living. For the first time in a very long time, I was really living in the moment. I started sharing beautiful recipes, and we journeyed through writing a beautiful book. I started teaching little cooking classes and workshops on the side. Michael had become such a wonderful self-taught food photographer.

I'll never forget that hope and pot roast go hand in hand.

Beer-Braised Chuck Roast with Red Onions

PREP TIME: *10 minutes* • BRAISING TIME: *5 hours* • SERVES: *4–6*

2 tablespoons butter

2 large red onions, sliced in thick, one-inch slices

1 3-pound chuck roast, nicely marbled with fat

Salt and pepper to taste (for most meats, 1 teaspoon salt per pound works nicely)

1 (12-ounce) medium-bodied beer, such as a pilsner or golden ale, not IPA

Preheat the oven to 300°F. Put the butter and onions in a large, oven-safe pot with a tight-fitting lid, and sauté over medium heat for 2 to 3 minutes. Place the roast on top of the onions. Season liberally with salt and pepper. Pour the beer into the pot, keeping the pour away from the meat so as not to disturb the salt and pepper. Cover the pot with the lid, and place in the oven for 5 hours. Check the meat periodically to make sure the liquid hasn't completely evaporated.

Sour Cream Smashed Potatoes

PREP TIME: *10 minutes* • COOK TIME: *45 minutes* • SERVES: *4–6*

3 to 4 pounds (10 to 12)
    Yukon Gold potatoes

1 cup sour cream

1 cup heavy cream (more if needed)

½ cup butter

½ cup milk

Salt and pepper to taste

Quarter the potatoes and place in a large pot, then cover with cool but not cold water. Bring to a rolling boil over high heat, then reduce to medium-high heat and a soft boil. Continue to cook over medium-high heat until the potatoes are easily pierced with a knife, 20 to 25 minutes. Drain the potatoes, then add back to the pot. Add the remaining ingredients. Smash the potatoes using a hand masher until the butter is melted and the liquid is absorbed (they will be chunky). Serve with the pot roast.

A Book for Sale with No Book

And but He said to me, "My grace is sufficient for you, for my power is made perfect in weakness." Therefore I will boast all the more gladly of my weaknesses, so that the power of Christ may rest upon me.

—(2 Corinthians 12:9, ESV)

The food at Minoela was fantastic, and shutting down the restaurant hurt, casting my love of cooking in a new, unsavory light. Cooking after Minoela closed was too raw. Cooking had always been a respite for me, and now it was this reminder of my hard reality. I felt like cooking stole things from me, and I was no longer inspired. I wanted to shut that part of me off in order to cope. After Minoela closed, I vowed I would never cook like that again. Cooking cost me my comfort and my home. Cooking almost cost me my marriage. If I am being honest, I now understand it wasn't cooking that had brought all those troubles, but it sure was a convenient scapegoat.

At home for dinner, after the restaurant closed, I was steadily cooking up unimaginative ground turkey and white rice and steamed broccoli. For breakfast, scrambled eggs and toast most days. The occasional spaghetti would round out the evening meals. I'd go to the grocery store with a list of staples that needed replacing. The budget was strict, and my imagination for cooking had seemingly run out. The same brands filled my cart month after month as I explored being a mother and wife. I no longer cooked for pleasure or excitement; I thought that part of my life was over.

Noah turned six months old. I'd been following his pediatrician's recommendations, introducing rice cereal and teething biscuits, and now, the doctor said, it was time to start him on solid foods!

Noah wasn't eating any of the traditional jarred baby foods I tried feeding him. The more expensive foods with organic veggies were far out of reach for my budget, but I splurged for a pouch of food from a line developed by a famous chef. It was zucchini and sweet potato, some fancy blend. I fed it to Noah.

Success! He loved it! But these blends were over two dollars a pouch. There was no way I could afford to buy them regularly for Noah. But I thought to myself, *Gosh, I can get zucchini on sale for a little over a dollar a pound and roast him some.* I did so, added a touch of olive oil, and puréed them. He loved them! So many servings for mere pennies!

I started making all Noah's foods. I'd go to the store and write down the combos from that fancy baby food line, then recreate them at home. Roasted zucchini and plums? All right! Noah gobbled it all up! I began making him quinoa with roasted veggies mixed into it. I hadn't even heard of quinoa before, but I found that you can buy it for a fraction of the cost in the bulk section compared to the fancy preportioned packages. I thought, *I bet he'd love real chicken stock in his rice.* I'd braise a whole chicken and feed him the tender, fall-off-the-bone meat along with rice and vegetables, all cooked in the stock. And he couldn't get enough!

Through this process, I started cooking again, and it felt like I was reborn. I'd scribble down delicious-sounding ideas and then work my budget around them. Mike was enjoying this turn too. I was still working as a makeup artist during the day, but I would think about what to cook for dinner at the makeup counter, then rush home to cook for the boys.

One day, Mike said, "You think you'd want to make pasta again?" I did! I didn't just *want* to make it; my soul *needed* to make it. I bought chives and tucked them into the dough like I'd always done at Minoela. It felt so good to create again. I started wondering if I should write all the old restaurant recipes down. It couldn't hurt. I sure didn't want to lose them!

Noah softened my heart toward myself, and he loved my cooking. We were poor but had so much during this time. Mike and I were learning to love each other again, being kinder to ourselves and our little family.

The only cookbooks I'd ever owned were a few Ina Garten books I'd received as gifts. I had a subscription to *Martha Stewart Living*, and I'd pore through the back issues daily just thinking about how I might someday write my very own book. I didn't know where to start or what it would take, but I knew I could cook. I've never been a hobbyist. I've always tried to make a living with my gifts and interests. I sold ice water to construction workers on my street as a kid, then candy out of my backpack as a teenager. My personality lends itself to big risks. It was never even a question that if I was going to write recipes down, they should become a book. It seemed like a natural next step. I love a good project, I love a good opportunity, and this is where I found myself: needing something to pour my creativity into. It felt right, but how to do it? I'd jump in and figure it out as we went.

One thing that brought me to life was looking at beautiful pictures of food. I knew every picture in Ina's books. I hardly read the recipes; I just pored over the photos. I'd clip out the pictures from *Martha Stewart Living*, never even looking twice at the recipe text. I'd drizzle olive oil just like the pictures or pile beans on toast as close as I could get it to the photos. If I was going to write a cookbook, I knew it'd have to be all about the food styling and photography. After many months of dreaming it up,

I called a friend from high school who worked as a professional photographer.

"Jeff!" I said. "I'd like to write a cookbook!"

He said, "Great. What kind of budget are you looking at?"

"Well, I don't have one, but maybe you'd take payments?" He said we should meet for coffee.

A few weeks later, I was sitting in a Starbucks, Noah resting in the crook of one arm, a few tattered magazines and a single Ina cookbook in the other. I explained that I didn't really know what I was doing, but I wanted to write a book. Jeff graciously began walking me through the process.

I started planning photo shoots for the first time. Jeff said, "Think of colors you like. Then buy the things that make you feel good. Colors like dark blue and natural wood photograph well."

Could I do this? I doubted myself every step of the way. I started visiting thrift stores to look for props. I'd shop using my grocery budget for the week, we would style and photograph my dishes, and then we would eat the meals for dinner. On one particular shoot, I gave Jeff a meager $125; I was embarrassed. We were making my lemon and Greek basil roast chicken. I had no money for the dish's ingredients. I called my sister and told her I needed a chicken, so she dropped off a chicken for me to roast. Mike carried the dining table outside to the flourishing courtyard beside our condo building. I placed the chicken in the middle as the centerpiece. Flies were landing on the chicken, and as Jeff photographed, I began to cry.

I must have looked like a madwoman. Who cries over flies? I waved them off, and the entire shoot felt tense. Jeff told me not to worry. "Just toss it afterward," he said. "It's the price of photography some days. The flies can be edited out of the shot."

But that wasn't why I was crying. The chicken was our dinner. After he left, I called my mom. I felt so broken. What was I doing? I told her we had no dinner now. I had been foolish and wanted to shoot outside, but the flies just wouldn't leave our dinner alone. She said, "You stop crying right now! You go and crank your oven up to 450 degrees, throw the chicken in, and enjoy your dinner. A couple of flies aren't going to ruin your evening or your meal." I felt this rush as I realized how right she was! I cranked the oven and baked the chicken for a while. It was fall-apart tender, and I'm sure every germ was killed in the heat. Sometimes we just gotta stop crying and crank the heat up.

It took two years to put the book together. I'd save up and pay Jeff when he arrived for that day's session. The shoots were painful. I'd get flustered and try to fit as much into one shooting session as I could. On summer days, we'd sweat through the shoots, just chipping away. In colder seasons, we'd bundle up and shoot on our front porch.

The wine-drenched short ribs were a porch shoot. I gifted them to Tom and Mary, neighbors I'd never spoken with before. They were a quiet couple who lived in the condo beside ours. They walked past our porch one day as we were shooting and mentioned how good it smelled. I noticed how frail Tom was. He must have been sick. We chatted a bit and wrapped up the shoot. As I packed up the brown butter carrots and short ribs, I decided to take some over to Tom and Mary. They were ecstatic and graciously accepted the dish of food.

Some weeks later there was a knock at my door. I was having a bad morning, fussing over plenty that likely didn't need fussing over. I answered the door, and Mary stood there pressing my white platter to her chest. Without her saying a word, somehow I knew. Tom had passed away, she said. She went on to tell me that the food I gave him was his last meal, a meal that he'd said was some of the best food he'd ever tasted. I hugged her, and we stood on my porch like that for some time. We wiped our tears, and as I closed the door, I knew in my heart we were doing something special through the creation of this food. I had never felt such honor in feeding someone. What a gift to be able to give food during such a difficult time.

This book had a very necessary place in my life. The process at every turn was healing my heart. I understood suddenly that everything wasn't about me. In fact, most things in life aren't about us, really, but about sharing with others. *My Heart's Table* was about sharing my life with other people.

We were near to bringing the project to a close when Jeff became sick with cancer and had to dedicate himself to that fight. As a result, he wouldn't be able to complete our little book. Mike stepped up and began teaching himself to use a camera. He was terrible at first, and so was I! We laugh now, but we'd fight over just how bad the photos were, and the only thing to do was take more photos and continue practicing. We didn't know it then, but he would end up pursuing photography seriously, making it into a career for himself. Every setback was a setup.

Jeff fought for his life for several years and has since made a full recovery. I will always be so grateful to him for being instrumental in getting my first book out there.

Once we neared the completion of the book, it was time to sell it! So simple, right? Wrong. I didn't know that publishers generally weren't interested in a completed work like mine—they wanted to be in on the idea from the very beginning so they could help bring the concept to life. I sent it out to a few publishers I found online. No one wanted it. I tucked it away for a year. Maybe I wasn't meant to sell it; maybe it was just for me. I was okay with that. During that year, folks would ask me if I was still working on my book. I'd change the subject. I wasn't working on it. I didn't know what to do.

One day, I thought, *Why not try to self-publish?* I started researching and decided we needed an editor, a graphic designer, and a platform to sell on. These services are wonderful and expensive.

I had recently started playing around on a new phone app called Instagram. Maybe I could offer my book to people out there. Maybe they'd buy a copy! I had three thousand followers when I started advertising *My Heart's Table*. I went through so many titles in my mind. I kept thinking, *What is this book about?* I thought I'd name it *The Simple Table.* After a few days, I thought that title may have been overplayed. I saw so much involving the words *simple* and *table.* I even started my Instagram handle as The Simple Table, and it just wasn't me. I asked myself who I was. Well, I think I make rustic food that's messy and comfortable, always with French and Italian influences. I make food that is full of fresh herbs and dripping with olive oil and flaky salt. I make food that cooks for hours until the perfect tenderness is achieved. It's joyful food. It's happy and full of life. My heart was pouring out at the time, and I can remember sitting in my mother's living room saying, "This book just feels like I'm pulling up to my heart's table." That was it.

I had no book, just pictures and a messy manuscript. But I began selling a book to people as a preorder. *Nonexistent book for sale—just $34.99!*

I presold one hundred books, and that was enough to pay the editor and the designer. We worked for a full year, and finally, in September 2014, we released *Rustic Joyful Food: My Heart's Table,* my first cookbook.

Look, sometimes you may lose your house. Sometimes you may lose all the food in your fridge. And your mom might have to buy you milk. Or you might have to get milk and juice with food stamps. I did. Sometimes, for cash to live, you sell your washer and dryer weeks before you move and must wash your clothes in the sink for a while. We did that.

Sometimes your tiny two-year-old will press his little face to the apartment window yelling, "Hey, they taked our car!" while you sob on the couch and tell him, "Yes, but we didn't need that car anymore. God gave us legs to walk." And that tiny toddler learns what "repo" means. Noah did.

You may lose friends; we left so many behind to heal. You may lose possessions. But please, my dear ones, never lose faith and hope. To me, Minoela meant "my gift." How little I knew what I would gain from all the loss. The gift wasn't in the material gain. The gift was fully loving myself right where I was—right where my family was. The gift was learning how to live outside of goals and achievements. To drink in daily life. The prize God had for our family was the restoration of my marriage and our first baby. We spent almost three years writing *My Heart's Table*. Those were my healing years. That book was my healing book.

Many years, many setbacks, many triumphs. Looking back, I can see how each hurdle and every struggle to publish the book was healing my heart. I was problem solving differently. I was growing more and more stable when storms came. I felt how much I could achieve if I just trusted the Lord to finish the steps at hand. I no longer planned things out so far in advance that I couldn't see the miracles as they happened. And I was grateful in a way I'd never felt before. Having so little but still being able to write and publish a book was a miracle that I felt I had very little to do with. God just asked me to put one foot in front of the other and to work on the next steps slowly and quietly.

The Instagram audience that followed along on the journey and purchased copies paved the way to an actual book release. I sold enough books to take our family to Disneyland. On release day, we had pulled together the money to buy plane tickets. We flew to California, packed peanut butter sandwiches, and spent the day at the park. I remember holding Mike's hand on Disneyland's Main Street and, with my phone, placing an order for my book on Amazon.

I once saw a picture of a tired miner. It was a cartoon drawing of him, exhausted, walking away from the digging he'd been doing. Just on the other side of the hill he was digging through was a pile of diamonds. Instead of breaking through to the other side, he gave up and walked away. We have a choice every day to give up. Or we can push through. I looked at that cartoon and related deeply. I was literally talking to the picture: *Don't give up, little guy. Look what's there, right where you are digging. You just can't see it yet. I know you are tired. I know you feel weary. But the treasure is just an inch away.* Don't give up on your breakthrough just before it comes.

"We did it, babe. We did it!" I cried of course. You know me—I always do. *My Heart's Table*, the book that healed my heart, was in the world.

I'm Learned Real Good

I didn't always know I was a writer. In fact, I barely graduated high school. I never took my studies seriously. I was too busy daydreaming about the injustices we faced as a student body, what I could do to earn money, or how to make my peers laugh at something I'd said.

I'll never forget being called into the front office and told by several members of the administration, who didn't particularly care for me, that I wouldn't be walking with my class at the graduation ceremony. I might still graduate if I completed summer classes, but I wouldn't be graduating alongside the rest of my class. My GPA just didn't cut it.

I felt like they had finally won. I sat across from a dreadful woman who delivered this news to me, clearly savoring every delicious bit as it left her mouth. Just a few weeks to go in my senior year of high school, and I was sunk. I went to my history teacher, a woman named Helen Fitzroy. If memory serves, I was set to receive a D in her class. Not passing. I told her I desperately needed to raise that grade. Could I please redo anything?

She agreed, although she didn't have to. My dad worked at the school as an administrator, and this may have encouraged her to show a little mercy. She liked me when many teachers did not. It's easy to not like the kid who is different or too loud or who has big ideas of her own and challenges everything. The kid who doesn't quite yet know what to do with the personality she was born with.

That was me. Too big for small people but never too big for my purpose in life. I studied during lunch breaks and after school, and I brought my history grade up. I graduated with a 2.4 GPA. I not only walked with my class, I delivered our final speech as the class president.

Mrs. Fitzroy changed my life. Many years later, I'd find myself starting over in life, picking up the pieces of my failed, beautiful restaurant, harboring a desire to write a book full of recipes. I'd barely turned papers in during high school, and I was rejected from the three colleges I applied to after high school. I didn't score well on my SAT exams. I wore this reality like a badge of honor, telling people that I wasn't book smart, but I was street smart, and that sure counts! It always garnered laughs, but I didn't feel very smart at all.

When I decided to write my first book, I couldn't shake this deep calling to share my story in the midst of the hardship I was living through. My husband and I were literally about to lose our home, and I began to write for the first time in my life at thirty years old. I wrote recipes and stories, and it felt good. I didn't know much about the mechanics of writing, but I knew everything about my heart and its feelings.

Of course, I got a job working in makeup after Minoela closed, returning to my roots as a makeup artist. And if there is one thing true of a woman who works in makeup, it's that she's likely got a side hustle. Makeup artists are wildly creative, intensely passionate, supportive folks. I've never in my life met a collective group of people who were so deeply creative and scrappy and loyal. My side hustle had become writing books and cultivating our new business, Rustic Joyful Food.

A friend at the makeup counter offered to edit my work. She was a paralegal at a law firm and said she edited all day long and would love to help. I was nervous. *Oh gosh, let someone read my messy recipes and poorly written essays?* I warned her that they were really messy, like I-don't-know-what-I'm-doing messy. At the time, I was doing some freelance food photography styling (another side hustle!) for a local magazine. The editor in chief had become special to me, for she saw past my green beginnings as a food stylist and offered wonderful advice, always followed by a "Meow." That's how she signed many of her emails—in cat phrases! I just adored her! She let me know early on in my book-writing process that I'd need to find an editor. My writing had a lot of strengths, but I'd need to invest in some help to polish it up.

So when my coworker offered, I said, "Okay!" I put the book onto a thumb drive and met her in a parking lot to hand it off. Several days passed. Then she called me. "Okay, I think I'm done," she said. "I want to start by saying you are *the best* makeup artist. Like, *the best*, girl! But honestly, I can't edit this. I think maybe recipes are above my pay grade."

She was kind. And she tried, but the book was a mess. She didn't have to say. I *knew* it. I felt defeated. I called a dear friend to tell her what happened, and she tried to let me down easy. "Maybe writing isn't for you," she said. "You've tried so many times to get this off the ground. Maybe it's okay to stop."

I felt very dumb. Why did I think I could I write a book if I didn't know how to write? Maybe authoring books *wasn't* for me. Maybe I'd just keep the book for myself and my family.

Soon after, I stopped into the office of the magazine I was freelancing for to say hello. My dear editor friend asked how the book was coming along. "It's not," I said. "I don't think I'm going to be writing it for a while. Maybe I need a break. I am having trouble finding an editor." I dared not tell her that my coworker couldn't even get through it.

She paused in thought. "You'll need Barbie," she said. "Here is her email address. She's not cheap but she's good. She's just what you'll need."

I waited a full month to reach out to Barbie. I didn't know anything about her, but I thought, *I'll just try*. I spent another few weeks going through what I'd written, working to clean it up as best I could.

Barbie, as it turned out, worked as a literary department head at a local university. I was terrified to contact her. I didn't get accepted into a four-year school, and I flunked out of community college because I couldn't get a handle on the math requirement. But I met Barbie in the cafeteria of the university where she worked. I was pushing my sleeping baby, Noah, in his stroller. She bought me coffee in a clear plastic cup. The knots in my stomach were making noise. I'd only ever dreamed of being accepted into a place like this. She agreed to take a look at my book. I gave her the same thumb drive I had handed off to the coworker who'd washed her hands of my mess. I explained to Barbie that I wasn't very smart but that I had this big desire to write and that I just didn't pay attention in school. I told her my grammar was terrible and that I was downright embarrassed to hand over my manuscript. I'd worked on it for months, just cleaning it up.

She slurped her drink and listened. I remember her fluffy hair had strands of silver in it. She had a long, kind face. With a half smile and twinkle, she said, "Let me be the judge of that."

We met for all of fifteen minutes, and just like that, Noah and I were off! I felt lighter. The university campus was so beautiful that I just pushed my baby around for a while to see it.

A few weeks later, she called. I remember talking over her

apologetically, letting her know, *I get it. It's so bad. Thanks for looking at it anyway.*

She said, "Danielle." I paused, barely daring to breathe. Then she said something I'll never forget: "Danielle, you are a beautiful writer. I was moved to tears by what you wrote. You just need a little help. That's where I come in. I'd love to take on this project. You're good!"

I was dumbfounded. And I needed Barbie. She taught me things as she edited my book (at a deep discount, taking payments over a year). She'd tell me the things she loved, and she quietly, brilliantly fixed my mess.

You see, we all need a Helen Fitzroy in our corner. We all need to find our Barbie. These women stood in a gap that was wide and difficult, and they believed in me. Barbie went on to edit my first two cookbooks. The lessons I learned in observing how she shaped my work are lessons I still draw from today. She used her editorial abilities to demonstrate that I had abilities of my own, and she set the stage for my career. Sometimes we need to just put one foot in front of the other where our dreams are concerned. And God will bring in the Helens and the Barbies at the perfect moment.

Don't for a moment doubt your calling because you aren't good enough *yet*. We only get better through starting and by trying. By believing who God says we are. We aren't meant to start out great. We gotta work and fall and fail our way upward. So get yourself out there. Even if you aren't good, you'll only be better for trying.

Mom Is Brave

In the second grade, I got the haircut of my dreams: a pixie cut with a rat tail. I was eight years old, and the world was my oyster! But we had a terrible neighbor kid nearby who mercilessly made fun of me.

He used to run out of his house yelling after me, "Hey! Is that kid a boy or a girl!" And my face would turn eight shades of red as I put my head down to walk faster past the bus stop.

My mom, bless her, said to me, "Okay, Danielle, next time he says that, you yell back, 'Bite the big one, jerk!'"

What a plan! This was it, my opportunity to really stick it to him. The next time I set out for the bus stop, here came the kid, flinging his screen door open to holler at me. Before he said anything, I squealed out with all my might, "BITE THE BIG ONE, JERK!"

A pause. I stood there. He said, "Wait...what?" Then he fell on the ground, laughing hysterically. "What does that even *mean*?" he cried, rolling around.

Our plan didn't work out too well. I reported back to my mom, and she said not to worry, that he'd stop. "You stood up," she said. She was right; that kid never bothered me again.

I was picked on a lot growing up. I used to think being singled out this way was a bad thing, that there was something wrong with me. But now I know it was because I was strong and that I have always stood out in my own unique way. I had a haircut no other second graders were getting; at fifteen, I wore a dress made for a forty-eight-year-old mother of the bride to my ninth-grade coed dance. When you step out of the box, things can get messy, but it's only then that you can uncover who you really are and freely discover the stuff—the *good stuff*—that really works for you. The pineapple upside-down cake of life!

My mom had very unconventional advice that worked for me. She was showing me that, metaphorically, there are many ways to bake a cake, and sometimes the good, gooey stuff is at the bottom, not in the pretty icing. Standing out, in other words, is good. The mother of my childhood memories is always wearing purple, gold, or green eyeshadow, and she lives in such a way that you can't help but see her confidence. She was the perfect mom for me.

I want to tell you that by simply being the mom you are right now, you are shaping your children into great humans. The difficult choices you make now are setting an example for your kids that will mean far more than anything you can tell them. You are doing a great job. You are doing the best you can with what you have, and if you aren't, then change it. You can pick out the things you don't like, the bad habits you've formed, and give them to God. Then move forward. That's all. Start right now. God made you a parent. God chose these kids for your care. Enjoy it, soak it in, and if you don't love it, pray to love it, because it's glorious.

I once had a friend tell me she couldn't wait till her kids were teenagers. "Then it'll be easy, and we will be friends," she said. "Nothing like these long nights and fits and being so tired that I can't fall asleep." I have to think she'd regret these words ten years on. One day, your kids are going to be young adults navigating strange, new terrain; how tragic if you could wish away the years leading up to that. Think of the joy you'd be depriving yourself of.

I close my eyes and see snippets of my childhood, and it's good. It's bold, it's uncensored, and it's real. And I learned things I can apply to motherhood now. Motherhood is bravery. Being alive isn't having everything prim, clean, and proper. It's messy, it's difficult, and it's stressful. But with each deep breath, you are reminded how much you are alive. You are raising tiny people.

Let me say it like this: You will fall short, you will stumble along the way and say awful things, but you *must remember* to start over each day, telling yourself that these *are* the good old days. These are the days you will wish you could have back years from now. When you are watching the baby you soothed all night wander into this great, big world, your heart will ache for yesterday. I pray you face forward with excitement while keeping in mind how wonderful and awesome being a mother is. I am growing up alongside my children. I still have outbursts and tantrums and sometimes think *that's not fair!* But when I really take time to cherish the beauty in each moment, each tiny hand, and every baby tooth, the splendor of this section of my life is revealed. I thrive in seeing wonder in my children's eyes.

We take family caravan road trip vacations each and every year, and it can be difficult slogging through the mountains with a crying baby in the back seat. But when we pause at the rest stop, take in the view and the heat, and get a snack from my dad's truck (he's the caravan leader, of course), memories are collecting in my brain, memories that are soothing, joyful, and comforting. I want to perfect the art of remembering this one simple fact: I'm going to miss this. You too are constantly making memories and living through moments you will long for. It's just how it is.

Imagine that the world is new, you haven't been hurt, you don't have deadlines, and your life is blameless. Imagine your job is to enjoy life, every moment. That's what our Heavenly Father desires for us: to rest and fully enjoy every moment. What a gift to demonstrate this for our children, to show them, wonder with them, teach them, and laugh with them. Cutting construction paper shapes, mixing cookies, and speaking to them in love is transformative. Reinforce their worth, and allow them to give in to their sense of sweet awe and wonder. I'm so grateful to have two boys experiencing the world for the first time, not through my tired eyes but with new, excited eyes.

It's no coincidence that the Bible gives careful instruction to receive Jesus with a childlike faith. To nurture our children is our primary job as mothers, but society sometimes paints another picture. In a world where society measures a good life by how much you possess or how many likes you've generated on social media sites, it's easy to lose sight of what matters. If you are lucky enough to become a mother, embrace it. Work with your children, and show them how life is meant to be lived: joyfully. Embrace the same patience our Father has for us. Rather than worry about tomorrow and the hurried pace of life, begin to look at things through your babies' eyes. Protect their hearts. Their time in our care is so short, and I promise you will miss the sleepless nights, the tears, the tiny hands that fit into your palm like a missing puzzle piece. Catch fireflies, run, pray, eat dinner together, build a fort, and make Popsicles, then sit on the back porch or the front stoop or look out your window and eat them together.

I know life is hard. Maybe you work full-time, maybe you're a single parent, or maybe you're tired and hurting. Ask God to heal your heart so the time you spend with your children is patient, pure, and kind. He makes all things new. I often feel like a bad mom. I can be short and sharp and overwhelmed by busyness. Writing this serves as a reminder even for myself that today is all we have. Some days, just skip school and head to the park or even a parking lot with a bike in tow for your kids to ride around on. They don't need fancy, perfect, or expensive. They were placed into your arms to love. They just want you. That's all. No fancy foods or expensive gifts will ever make you a better mom; *you* are all they need right now, and you have everything you need to provide a loving childhood.

Life is like pineapple upside-down cake. All the good bits are at the bottom, and you gotta flip it over to find them. Start flipping, and get into today, because tomorrow is too far away. Now is the time.

Pineapple Upside-Down Cake

Adapted from Betty Crocker

PREP TIME: *15 minutes* • BAKE TIME: *38–45 minutes* • SERVES: *8–12*

1 cup melted butter, divided

1 cup dark brown sugar, packed

1 (20-ounce) can pineapple rings
   in juice

1 (8- to 12-ounce) jar maraschino
   cherries, drained and stems removed

1 box yellow cake mix

4 eggs

1 teaspoon vanilla extract

Preheat the oven to 350°F. Pour ½ cup melted butter into a 9-by-13-inch pan, then sprinkle the brown sugar over the butter. Arrange the pineapple rings evenly in the pan, reserving the juice. Arrange the cherries in and around the pineapple rings.

Combine the cake mix, eggs, vanilla extract, remaining butter, and reserved pineapple juice in a mixing bowl. Mix until smooth, and pour evenly over the pineapple rings. Bake for 38 to 45 minutes, until the cake is just set in the center (when a pick is inserted, it should have bits of cake crumbs but no streaks of batter). Allow to cool for 2 to 3 minutes, then turn the cake out onto a large platter or cookie sheet. Serve warm with ice cream.

The Thistle and the Currant

Last year for Mother's Day, Mike and Noah gave me the most magnificent red currant bush. She grew these beautiful strands of glassy-red berries and soft, green, almost heart-shaped leaves. I put this perfect little berry bush in a nice big pot and waited every day for the strands of berries to ripen.

One day, just before the berries were ripe for picking, I approached the bush to discover that a deer had wandered onto my porch and eaten the delicate bush down to nothing. I cried. I was looking forward to those two tiny berry strands. In my disappointment, I just left the plant on my porch and let a thistle move into the pot right next to what was once my glorious currant bush.

Every day, that thistle grew bigger and stronger. I kept thinking,

I should pull the thistle. But I never did. Life got busy, as it does, and almost a year went by. Every few days, I thought about yanking that thistle out, but I didn't. Eventually, when the thistle had grown to about two feet in height, I braved the thorns and got right down to the base and began to pull. But when I got it out, the currant came up as well. The thistle had managed to wind its gnarly roots around the currant's roots. I untangled them, and after deliberating whether to cast both weed and plant out entirely, I repotted the currant.

Two weeks later, much to my disbelief, I saw tiny bits of green around the currant. I carefully packed more soil and mulch around the base and began watering it again. Sure enough, the two tiny sticks sprouted small leaves and tiny clusters of flowers that would become fruit in time.

This little plant really made me think. Last year, I had wanted those two little strands of berries. I gave up after the deer ruined it. I allowed a terrible, bitter weed to take root after the tragedy. That thistle root got deeper and bigger and threatened to kill the currant off for good. I can't help but relate to this story in such a real way. When life doesn't go as planned and we face hardship and disappointment and loss and grief, tiny weeds move into our hearts. Weeds that grow bigger and stronger with each day, threatening to choke out our hope and joy and rob us of our peace. Only Jesus can rid our hearts of the unwanted bitter roots. Only our savior can rebuild what was lost.

The currant plant ultimately grew healthier and more

productive than it had ever been before. It provided loads of berries after its raw and bitter fight with the weed. The thistle almost won. It seemed to have finished off what the deer had left incomplete. It was only after removing the weed that the plant could begin to really heal.

If we would simply ask the Lord to remove every bitter root in every area of our lives that is holding us back from growing, He so gently and tenderly will. He will heal every broken place in our hearts. I've had, and continue to have, a lot of broken places in my heart and mind that the Lord has been healing. Lots of thistles being removed in a lot of areas where I let tiny weeds take root.

Each day, I am growing stronger and healthier where the tiny weeds of life's hardships and disappointments once sprouted. I am asking the Lord to continue to heal the broken places. Ask the Lord this moment to reveal and begin removing weeds and, where the thistles once were, to begin repacking healing soil around your heart. You will flourish again, just as the glorious currant did. You will come back stronger with dozens of strands of glassy berries in areas that were once barren and desolate. You are designed to rebuild; you are designed to thrive.

Boston

For me, food hasn't really ever been about how delicious something was. The more I think about food and what it means to my soul, it's always the emotion running alongside whatever I'm eating that stands out. We've been taught for so long that emotional eating is wrong, that it's a crutch. The world tells us that attempting to feed our emotions will lead to indulgence, shame, and unhealthiness. Of course, some of these sentiments ring true. But what if we allowed ourselves the joy associated with food?

Food carries with it so many elements we often barely consider. I eat so many meals these days that are associated with powerful, lovely memories. But not all memories tied to food are happy ones. Sometimes a memory that is painful or bittersweet can link itself with a particular meal because it's a reminder of a loved one who has passed on or moved away, but there is a certain beauty in this as well. You can, in a very tangible way, re-experience the past through food. There is also something simply splendid about satisfying hunger; when we are hungry for food or love or companionship or a break or grace, once we've been given what we are hungering for, there is a period of calm and feeling loved.

While I was in Boston on a solo work trip recently, I missed my husband desperately. I kept thinking, *I wish he could see this. I wish he could walk these streets and laugh with me.* I wanted him to see, and I wanted to know that he could feel what I was feeling. The value of alone time is not lost on me, and it's healthy and won-derful to be alone and lean into God. It's an experience I treasure. But on this particular Boston evening, I missed Mike. Trying to get out and see the city, I went to a bar for my very first lobster-in-a-restaurant experience. I don't mean a minuscule lobster tail served beside an eight-ounce steak fillet, now. I've done that before, and it's fantastic. I mean full-on, cold-water, pulled-from-the-North-Atlantic-just-a-stone's-throw-away-eight-hours-ago *lobster*, intact, claws on, served straight-up, steamed, with a nutcracker and a vat of melted butter. In short, the stuff dreams are made of.

The evening went a little something like this: An excruciat-ingly long line of people waiting to be checked in by the hostess. A packed bar to the left and a packed house in the dining area to the right. I waited nearly an hour just to work my way up to the hostess stand. "Table for one!" I shouted. The music was loud, and the air smelled like a bar, naturally.

The hostess leaned in and shouted back, "We don't seat parties of one! Head to the bar."

I glanced over at this nightmarish option, then told her, "I want to order a lobster!"

She said, with finality, "Order it at the bar!"

It was late, I was hungry, and things weren't looking good here. I beheld the crowd of drunken, happy people with beers in their hands. The bar was so busy—totally packed. They didn't seat parties of one? Really? The bar looked like a war zone, full of wanton lovers battling for attention. I hadn't pushed my way into a meat market like this since my early twenties. It was chaos: loud music and wall-to-wall people sloshing drinks. Not one person in the bar was eating any food.

"Surely you can squeeze little married thirty-six-year-old me into the dining area, can't you?" I pleaded. She shook her head. In the bar, dude bros and lone wolves scanned the room, hoping to catch someone's eye. I tried to reason with this immovable rock of a hostess. "C'mon, I'm too old for this. Lemme just get a lobster. It's my first time in Boston!"

She leaned in and shouted over the noise, "It's the bar or nothin'. Sorry!" With her thick Boston accent, *sorry* came out *saaary*.

I turned to leave, dejected, then stopped.

Nah, I was gonna do it. I squirreled my way through the mob to the bar. Folks waved credit cards, shouting drink orders at the bartenders. *Man*, I thought, *I do not miss this scene*. I wiggled my way up, and after determining that waiting patiently for my turn wasn't going to gain any traction here, I ended up aggressively taking my turn. "I want a lobster!"

"Here?" the girl behind the bar said.

"Yup!"

She said, "One, two, or three pound?"

I said, "Three pounds." She looked surprised. "In my defense," I said, "most of the weight's in the shell, right?"

She pointed at a bar back. "Get that lady a stool!" She wiped my patch of the bar and squirted water into a plastic cup from a foot away.

I just sat there, waiting. *Why am I doing this?* There were so many people here, not on their phones, legitimately looking for a date, for love. After twenty minutes, my lobster came out. It was massive. There was a tiny side salad and this mammoth beast of a crustacean, piping hot and accompanied by a big ol' bowl of butter.

Thirty seconds before, I had been invisible, but now I was on Front Street. Not a single other person in this bar was eating or even sitting down. I felt a twinge of loneliness. Man, here I was, and I just wanted my husband to be here with me. This sort of stuff was meant to be shared; this experience was the kind of thing we should be doing together. I wasn't supposed to be eating this lobster alone. I hesitated a bit, then thought, *Okay, here goes. I'm enjoying this even if it's a rough setting.*

The bar area was getting more crowded by the moment, and

people were absolutely watching me at this point. But this was basically my dream: just me and a lobster the size of my arm. No forks (I don't know why I didn't think to ask for one), I just dug in and started making quick work of the lobster. More and more people began staring. A guy came up and said, "You're a badass. No beer for me. Gimme the lobster!" I felt like a hero.

Two girls worked their way over, and one of them said, "You know, you're just tearing into that lobster right here, and now we want a lobster!"

Now, instead of awkwardness, my bar lobster was sort of a celebration, like, *oh yeah, you can totally do that!* This is a lobster restaurant, right? I drew plenty of attention and was covered in butter. I finished my dinner, and an older woman slipped right into my seat as I stood up, her husband at her side. She said, "You've got the right idea. We saw you waiting from the restaurant side. We want the same thing you had!"

I closed my tab and worked my way back through the crowd, feeling a little proud. I walked to the back of the restaurant to wash up—wet naps can only take buttery hands so far. I really started thinking about this lobster and what it meant. I eat alone in every city I work in, and I don't mind. It's become very normal for me. Sometimes I even prefer dinner by myself to gather my thoughts and clean house mentally. But this lobster was different. I'd just had this funny, strange experience, but I couldn't high-five anybody about it. I went back to my hotel room alone, and with the time difference and kids in bed back at home, it was too late to even call Mike and tell him about it right afterward. The one thought I had on repeat while tearing into that massive beast of a lobster was, *I wish my darling friend was with me.*

Are the wonderful experiences we have as wonderful if we aren't able to share them, laugh about them afterward, and relive them from time to time when a breeze brings the memory sailing back in? I want to share everything with Mike, everything that makes me laugh and cry, the things that make me whole, that tear my heart up. We have beautiful children together, born out of choosing to love each other more than all our struggles and all our differences. He is my sweetest friend and my biggest champion. The experience of living, with all its ups and downs, with all its beautiful messiness, is something I want to share with this man, always.

You see, Mike has never been responsible for my happiness. His job is only to be my partner, to share this life and adventure together. Whenever I see a lobster, I'm reminded of sharing and of that wild night in Boston when all I wanted to do was experience that dang lobster in that crowded bar with my best friend. We don't have a conventional life with access to lots of babysitters and a regular dating schedule. In fact, it used to pain my heart that I didn't have a normal dating life with my husband. We work together, and we always work forty-two jobs to make it add up, and everyone everywhere seems to agree: *You must date your spouse! You must fit the mold and prioritize your marriage, or you will grow apart.* That's all well and good, but sometimes circumstances make standing

Tuesday night dates harder to come by; sometimes you have to get creative. You have to work with what you have to set aside time for your souls to connect.

We forgive each other the things that need forgiving. We are on this wild ride together, and simple forgiveness is one of the keys to happiness. I'll share my life with Mike until the wheels fall off and until forever comes. He's my lobster for this whole life, and I'll be his. He's given all the meaning in the world to my work and the books we write and the life we live. Marriage can be very difficult and even very lonely sometimes, but remember that those seasons change. Never stop trying, never stop eating together, and never fail to share your heart.

When I think back to Boston and the packed bar, feeling wildly insecure about cracking open a crustacean the size of Rhode Island alone, I remember desperately wanting to share it with Mike. I know I needed to be there alone to know I *could* be alone and find joy. We are made to do awkward things. We can survive lonely times. I was miserable at first, but those feelings turned to pride as I walked back to the bathroom to wash up. I really did that, all by myself, three thousand miles from home, at midnight. Maybe you don't have a life lobster yet or yours has gone away. Don't forget to cherish the times you make it through the awkward stuff with just you and God. He's always going to be there, cheering you on and pushing you through. You can do amazing things by yourself. That's when God speaks to me, always by myself. Always remember, order the lobster in the bar.

Don't Give Up. Just Learn to Rest

Please be kind to the woman you are. She's been through an awful lot. She is walking a road to find contentment and joy. She isn't a job title. She isn't a culmination of all her career success. She is fearfully and wonderfully made, full of life and specific gifts that make her a unique and beautiful addition to the world.

It's funny how we walk into parties or meet people for the first time and ask strangers the question "What do you do?" We wear our jobs like our identities. Our jobs are an aspect of our existence, certainly, but there are some questions I try to ask myself regularly to make sure I'm walking in the right direction. Am I kind? Am I generous? Do I work to make people feel good?

And what does it mean to be a "success"? How does that relate to pursuing your passions? How do we even find out who we are supposed to be? Spoiler alert: You were born who you are supposed to be, and your job is to take life on as a journey, not a destination. That's a tall order.

I've always believed long-term success comes down to making thousands of tiny daily choices: making your bed each morning, folding and putting away the clean laundry, washing the dishes and cleaning up the kitchen each night. Making these small choices lays the groundwork for the bigger decisions to be made in the other areas of our lives. Perhaps we even fail at maintaining this kind of discipline on most days, but it's important that we *don't give up*. I think we all start out believing there is this magical formula. Do these things and voilà: happiness and rainbows and you've achieved your dreams!

The truth is that most success is hard-won. If you had asked me in my twenties what success means to me, I'd have had plenty to tell you: houses, cars, vacations, money in the bank, food in the fridge. After life got my attention, I came to realize that those things don't equal success for me any longer. Success to me now is so wildly simple. It's a healthy, loving marriage and healthy, happy kiddos. It's loving myself through the storms that come into my life. It's leaning fully on Jesus for strength and comfort. It's humility and forgiveness. Real success is won in ways most people will never see. The quiet actions like helping others, praying for people. Or dedicating my time and resources in ways that are private and small and known only to a few.

Through this understanding and articulation of success, I've been able to pursue my calling. But how do you know what you are called to do? How do you find your passion?

I was all of nineteen, sitting in a night class during my freshman year of college. As a class, we were all discussing what we wanted to be. The professor asked each of us to write down five things we'd do for free, things we *loved* to do, that, if money were not a factor, we would do happily for the rest of our lives. We all scribbled. Then, when the exercise was finished and the class was quiet, he said, "Somewhere on that page is your calling. Now go figure out how to do one of those things and make money doing it."

I wish I still had that paper, because I honestly don't remember what I wrote down. But I never forgot what he said. I've thought about it many times in my life. Working at a job I didn't particularly love or feeling lost in my choices, I would think about that class exercise. *Now go figure out how to do one of those things and make money doing it.* I've come to realize that, for me, this sentence has nothing to do with any particular job I might hold. We all work at jobs to pay bills and carry on with the living of our lives, and the job, whatever it may be, is a worthwhile means to an end. But being able to give to people and donating resources are my passion, and fortunately my job accommodates that.

There is beauty in the everyday, in waking up and heading to work and working hard while you are employed by whomever. There is no such thing as a dead-end job. You are just where you are to learn and grow for a bigger purpose until it's time to move on. You learn what you do and don't want while at work. I know we are meant to be many things in the course of life. There is no *one special thing* we are supposed to do; we will wear many hats and serve different purposes at various times. This is difficult, but it teaches lessons and builds character. Learning to navigate choppy waters is of far greater value than smooth sailing. Do not choose to live in a bubble of fear either. It's okay to step out in an area where you aren't qualified if you feel called to it. We are inadequate, we aren't good at everything, and we are designed this way, to fully need a savior. We will never be fully adequate aside from Him. There is so much freedom in embracing that!

Even if you're afraid, try something new and ask for help. You don't have to be an expert to do something you love. We all start out just loving something and trying to figure out how to make a little money at it. I think that kept me from stepping out earlier in ways I knew my heart was called to. I wasn't good enough, so I held back. I've come to learn that we get good enough once we *get started*. That's how we grow.

I knew from a young age that my purpose in life was to minister to people, to love people. I just didn't know what that looked like. I went to a youth conference when I was thirteen years old, and a man told me that, one day, I'd speak to the masses, particularly to women. I tucked that promise away and never forgot it. I am many things. I am a writer and a food stylist and a speaker and an actor who plays herself on television. I was very bad at all those things when I started. I just didn't give up on me.

I've heard many women say that they've lost themselves to motherhood. Or they've lost themselves to a dead-end job or terrible marriage. The truth is that you are still you; you just took a different route, and it's okay to reevaluate and figure out what you need to do to fix things up and pivot along with the Lord's guidance. When we lost our restaurant, home, and car, I thought, *I ruined everything.* I did fail at that endeavor, but that failure set me up for a beautiful and rewarding career in food, one where I'm focused on helping people love their lives while cooking delicious, wholesome meals.

You don't have to make any decisions alone, ever. Prayer really works. It feeds the soul with hope. Did you know that you are designed for hope? Don't for one moment think you've missed your calling, that you are too old or too inexperienced. You are right where you need to be. Get your hopes up.

Let each day be an opportunity to make a small choice or take a step toward changing your life if you want to. Register for one class with the aim of finishing your degree. Start walking fifteen minutes a day for heart health. Dump that soda addiction. Make a list! What do you want to do? What ignites your soul and fills your heart with joy? Don't forget to love where you are right now. I'm not talking about toxic positivity, where everything is okay all the time. I'm talking about breathing in and finding some joy mixed in with the hard stuff and loving the woman you've always been.

I mess up daily. There is comfort in knowing my identity will never be defined by who I think I am or what my job title happens to be. It's actually in who God says I am. I am made, you are made, in the image of God, created for a purpose. And maybe part of fulfilling that purpose has you mothering and working at a bank, grocery store, or restaurant. Whatever you choose, don't ever feel bad about the choice. If you don't love it, think of one thing you can do to find contentment in the job. Or figure out one or two things that might change up where you are right now altogether.

Our paths aren't meant to be easy. Some folks take years and years to get to where they'd like to be. When we started Rustic Joyful Food, I had no end goal, but I had this desire to love people and teach them how to cook. With that one desire, I was able to choose something small each day, whether it was writing a recipe or posting to Instagram or writing to a company and asking to freelance for them. I just made sure I achieved at least one small thing each day. That pattern led me to teaching workshops and writing *My Heart's Table*.

After five years of working on Rustic Joyful Food, I found myself growing weary. It was a nice creative outlet, but we weren't making much money, and it took up a lot of time. Mike and I were visiting a friend whose husband owned a real estate firm. He had been asking me to work for him for years. "I'll make you richer than you could ever dream," he said. I swam in their pool, honestly thinking maybe it was time to let Rustic Joyful Food go.

We ate dinner. I was very transparent with them. I told them I just didn't know if I'd be happy selling houses. But I could be. I could be happy anywhere, especially if it meant I was providing for my family. Perhaps Rustic Joyful Food had run its course. We were in a lull. At the time, I was trying to sell my first self-published cookbook, and things felt difficult. I cried when we left.

I thought long and hard about letting Rustic Joyful Food go. *When is it going to get easier?* I thought. There was this small voice inside me urging me not to quit but maybe rest awhile.

I rested. I worked my job, but I never let Rustic Joyful Food go. I never took up real estate. I thought about it often, especially when things got difficult financially. I never had this fervent "NO!" in my heart, and I know that God would have honored my work, but it just didn't feel right.

So I held on to Rustic Joyful Food. As of this writing, Rustic Joyful Food is ten years strong. It's not who I am, but it's a way for me to walk in my gifts and carry out my calling to minister to people and love them. And I happen to make delicious food while doing it! Not quitting has brought blessings into my life. Resting and checking in with the Lord often has brought blessings. I don't think we ever *arrive*; I think we are meant to keep moving toward authenticity.

The Bible teaches that the world will make room for our gifts. You don't need to be something grand; you just need to move forward with the Lord. Find things each day that you like about who God made you to be, and don't focus so much on who *you* think you should be. I promise the world will open up. Scribble down those things that light your soul on fire, for those gifts will make a way for you. God will make a way for you. It won't always be easy, but just go easy on yourself. Lean on Him when you can't quite hold yourself up. He's writing your story. You are called for His glory. Don't give up. Just learn to rest.

Boiling Ice

You aren't supposed to be good at everything. I think most of us know this intellectually, but it's often something that has to be believed in our hearts before we truly accept it. Having grace for ourselves and our bodies and our actions is a tall order, difficult to master. To really live in your skin, to be aware of your strengths and weaknesses and try to navigate each day playing to your strengths, isn't easy. And asking for help in the areas where you are weak isn't easy either. At times, it can feel almost impossible.

If you are like me, you might dream of help but have no set method or design for asking for it. I don't want to be a bother to folks, and I don't want to look weak. I've gotta pretty much have it together all the time. This isn't something I'm proud of. I'm often the helper to those who need help. I will drop everything and bring you dinner, drive your aunt to her doctor appointment, or come clean your bathroom...but I struggle asking for things I need.

This past winter, it snowed where we live. Snow is beautiful. It's soft and powdery and lays a pristine blanket over all it falls upon. It never ceases to amaze me how the world looks brand-new under the cover of snow. My boys are at prime snow-loving ages, and this year, we've been embracing the snow. Growing up, I couldn't get enough! I'd play until my clothes were soaked and my fingers numb. My mom would make popcorn and hot choco-late to warm us up after sledding for hours. We'd even sneak into the backyard of an empty house nearby and slide down the hill at night in a giant metal mixing bowl.

This year, when the blanket of snow came to western Washington, I called my sister and asked to come play. We suited up to go play in the snow with the cousins. I had a few nerves, as we aren't built for snow around here. We get six inches, and the world stops. It's winter storm watch, and it usually snows a maxi-mum of three times each winter, here for a day or two, then gone.

Jenny lives twenty minutes due south, just across the street from my parents' house, and you'd think it was another country. They always get *much* more snow than in our neighborhood, so we were geared up for some winter fun. Mike didn't want to go, thinking the roads would be too treacherous. It was 24 degrees outside, and driving in the snow doesn't exactly excite us. But our kids needed some of that same magic we had growing up, so off we went. The main roads weren't too bad after all, but the lakeside drive my sister and parents live on is only used by the residents, so the snow and slush were deeper, thicker, and a little slippery.

My parents' house is directly across the road from my sister's house, on a downward slope. We pulled off the road to park on the shoulder adjacent to the wrought-iron fence enclosing my parents' property. What were we thinking? The car began to slide toward the fence, tires spinning as Mike tried to correct. I gasped and squeezed Mike's arm. The fence was just a couple of feet away. My heart was racing. My mom would be so upset! All of a sudden, I was ten years old again, and I didn't want to ruin Mom and Dad's fence!

We didn't hit the fence, but the car was stuck. We all got out and ran through a foot of snow up to my sister's house. My sister fell right in line, and we agreed: *don't tell Mom!* We were both kids again at this point, laughing at first but becoming increasingly nervous.

"Put pots of boiling water on, and we'll melt the snow around the tires!" she suggested.

"Okay, great idea!" We got a shovel. The work began. For ten minutes, we shoveled snow from around the tires and shuffled pots of boiling water back and forth between the kitchen and the car. Sloshy mud was the only thing happening. The tires spun, and the car slid even closer to the fence.

I started to cry. Mike and I were full-blown fighting at this point. I stood in the middle of the road, begging Mike to just try and back up the car. He hollered back all the reasons why it wouldn't work. My mom was gonna kill me! I was soaked, and the car just wouldn't budge in the right direction. Just then, my mom came out of her house. "What are you guys doing?"

"We're stuck," I hollered, "sliding toward your fence." I expected the worst. I expected my mom to be furious.

She said, "Okay, well, just let the kids play, and your dad will get you out when you are ready."

Anxiously, I said, "We are ready now." The last forty-five minutes had been hellish! I wanted to go home. Meanwhile, the kids were squealing and laughing up on the property behind me.

"No," she said. "Your sister made lunch. Just go play." She clearly didn't understand how bad it was!

My dad came out onto the front porch and said, "Don't worry about it, babe! Holler when you are done playing, and I'll tow you out."

I trudged back to my sister's house, worried and dejected. *Wait till they see what a mess we're in. No way they can pull us out.* About five minutes later, Mike appeared at my sister's back door, soaked and looking unworried. He took a sip of coffee and said, "We're out!"

I was shocked. "Uh, what do you mean we're out?"

"Your dad," Mike said, "felt bad that you were crying and said, 'Gosh, I don't know why she's so upset.' He threw two old carpet remnants down behind the rear tires, and I drove right out. I found a level space to park, and it took all of three minutes."

Over the past hour, I had lost all my peace. I cried and fought, and my efforts were met with defeat. I had no idea we could get out so easily. I relied on my own understanding of the world to help me and had failed miserably. Isn't it funny how sometimes we would rather fail miserably on our own terms than ask for help?

A quick phone call to my dad would've changed our entire afternoon. "Hey, Dad, I'm stuck."

"No problem. I have this thing called life experience, and I know just how to get you out."

Often in life, we don't ask God for help. We try forty-five things before we go to Him with our worry, our doubt, our disbelief. We think *If I can just try this first…* We end up exhausted, spun up, and defeated. His yoke is easy, and His burden is light. Don't waste another moment splashing boiling water under your tires in hopes it'll free you from the slippery ice. Just go to the source.

My mom called me as I ate lunch and calmed down. "It's just a fence, sister," she said. I love it when my mom calls me "sister." It's this calming, kind thing I've loved since I was a little girl. "Even if you did slide into it, we'd just get it fixed."

How soft and simple is the answer waiting from our Heavenly Father if we'd just go to Him and ask. The way out of the ice and snow was still messy and took effort, but it didn't have to start how I planned. If there is something you need, even if you are ashamed or scared, just ask Him to take over. I guarantee He's got a few carpet remnants to throw down for you to drive right on out.

Line 'Em Up

Noah was just a baby. We stood in the front doorway, waving good-bye to Mike, who was leaving for a couple of days to photograph a location wedding. This was our first time away from each other for any extended time since Noah had been born. I had a baby in a new apartment in a new city. The only person I knew here was Earl, the apartment manager who worked the front desk in the community office. We'd just lost our house a few months prior, following our bankruptcy, and were in full-on starting-over mode. Our life felt simple and slow and hard, but it had taken on such deep meaning, although I couldn't quite see it at the time.

On that October evening, it was pouring, like monsoon rain-ing, as I watched Mike's taillights fade off down the road. I was a little nervous to be caring for Noah alone, even for a couple of days. Noah and I had been sick that whole week. I'd just begun to feel a little better, and my appetite was coming back. I remember I had a whole chicken in the freezer, which I set out to defrost. I had a jar of Spanish green olives and a cupboard full of dried spices. Noah loved to eat rice, and I thought I'd make us a chicken dinner. I always make a chicken when under the weather, whether I feel sick, blue, or just plain in need of deep comfort. Something about a roasted chicken with a little onion just seems to make things all right. Add to it a little prayer, and a chicken for dinner during hard times is medicine I can count on.

There was a ladies' conference happening at the church we attended before moving, and they'd just introduced livestreaming. I logged on to watch. I had been feeling out of sorts for some time that year. There had been so much change. Being a new mom in a new city in a fairly new marriage, I had so many emotions I wasn't dealing with well—just life stuff, I thought. My eyes were teary quite a bit. We were striving to make ends meet as best we could, but life felt difficult. So sitting on the couch and loading up the livestream, I was fully prepared to soak in the Word being spoken at the ladies' conference.

Our home smelled wonderful as the chicken cooked. There are few things as satisfying as a quiet house and the scent of the dinner you prepared hours ago wafting through the air, a comforting reminder that the next meal is handled. I braised the chicken with the Spanish green olives, paprika, turmeric, and a trusty can of tomatoes. That smell of the toasted spices wafted through our little house, and I kept thinking it smelled more incredible than it should, considering how little it cost me. The chicken was a couple of dollars. The seasonings I had had on hand for some time. All of it mixing with the chicken drippings...it was glorious. I couldn't wait to sop up the juices with a bit of buttered bread. Glorious comfort food!

I find the best foods are slow and humble. They cook in a way that isn't flashy but timeless. I serve the chicken, fall-apart tender in bright red, oily broth, over jasmine rice. Jasmine rice smells like buttered popcorn while it cooks, and I learned that you could buy a pound for just a dollar in the bulk section at my grocery store. I dished our food up in one bowl. I sat on the couch and fed Noah bites from my plate. I loved how, when he was small, he never wanted his own plate; he just loved eating bites from mine. A cartoon played in the background, and I took in the livestream from the laptop sitting on my little coffee table.

The speaker began, and I was enjoying her words. At one point, she told all the women watching to close their eyes. Then she asked us to visualize and line up every person who had ever wronged us, to stand before every person who'd hurt us or dragged us through some sort of hell.

"Now, forgive them," she said. "You see, you won't always get an 'I'm sorry,' but you still need to move on. And by actually forgiving people who hurt you, you will be completely set free from hurt and bitterness."

Rain hitting my living room window. Cartoons playing for Noah. Shredded chicken and rice with green olives. And forgiveness. This memory is still so vivid for me.

When we go through traumatic experiences—being lied to, fired from jobs, broken up with in marriages and friendships—we collect these battle scars. Quietly, the scar partly heals, but we move forward a little wounded. That wound begins to affect our daily lives before we are even aware of it. Forgiveness has a healing power that almost nothing can touch in terms of effectiveness. Even if you never get an apology, you gotta line 'em up and forgive 'em. Even if your side of the story is never heard, you gotta line 'em up and forgive 'em.

I closed my eyes and lined all the people up, and one by one, I forgave. I had been carrying burdens. So many people had hurt me, and I knew it affected me deeply. I began envisioning situations and people that I hadn't thought about in a long time. I started saying out loud, "I forgive you. Lord, help me to forgive people who hurt me." Then I pictured myself. "I forgive you," I said.

Sometimes we aren't very kind to ourselves. I ate the chicken and rice and listened to her preach, and more folks kept coming to mind. Every one of them received a relieved, imaginary I forgive you. The more I forgave, the better I felt. Unforgiveness is sneaky. It's the story you tell over and over to illustrate a point. It's the way you think about a place or event where you felt wronged, and it plays out repeatedly in your mind with a new intensity each time you relive it to share it with others. We don't have to live this way.

We can choose to work on it, to let it go with God's help. I believe we can't achieve much without the Holy Spirit truly helping us through it.

What a relief this was! What a joy not to carry that burden anymore. An easy feeling entered the room. A shift began from this point forward. Forgiveness didn't happen overnight, and I still had to remind myself to let things go, but this experience changed how I carried burdens.

Ever since, I *often* work to get in a deep, gritty heart check-in with the Lord to see if I'm hiding away any unforgiveness. It's uncomfortable, and I am wrong a lot. Unforgiveness turns into bitterness, and that gives way to anger and stress. I ain't got no time for any of that mess! I'll lay awake in bed and ask the Lord to reveal things that are hiding in my heart, ways of thinking that are holding me back. He is faithful in revelation, not always in that instant but when the time is right. You see, it's not all about me and my feelings. It's infinitely valuable to live like the world doesn't revolve around our feelings of hurt or shame or rigidness. The world is much kinder when we forgive ourselves and others. My mother always reminds me that I need to allow others to be as free as I expect to be. This lesson especially hits home for me in the area of forgiveness.

That evening, I received some of the best advice I've ever been given. Line 'em up, forgive 'em, and keep on truckin'. It's time: forgive 'em.

Spanish-Style Braised Chicken

PREP TIME: *10 minutes* • BRAISING TIME: *2½–3 hours* • YIELD: *4 generous servings*

2 to 3 tablespoons olive oil	1 tablespoon ground turmeric
1 Spanish yellow onion, sliced	1 tablespoon onion powder
1 (6-ounce) can tomato paste	1 whole chicken, quartered
2 cloves fresh garlic, crushed	2 cups pitted green olives of your choice
1 tablespoon ground coriander	Salt and pepper to taste
1 tablespoon ground paprika	4 cups unsalted chicken stock or water

Preheat the oven to 325°F. Coat the bottom of an enamel-covered Dutch oven or ovenproof stewing pot with lid with the olive oil. Lay in the onion slices. Add the tomato paste, garlic, and spices, then sauté over medium heat 2 to 3 minutes. Place the chicken in the pot, breast side down, and add the olives. Season with salt and pepper. Add the stock or water to the side of the pan; this will ensure you don't rinse the salt and pepper from the meat. Place in the oven to braise for 2½ to 3 hours. Remove the lid, and increase the heat to 425°F for the last 25 minutes. Serve over jasmine rice or with warm bread for sopping up the rich broth.

I Burned It

I mean, I really burned it. I was scrubbing the kitchen down and preparing for an online Zoom cooking class. *Yes, you'll need to get that caramel started*, I thought to myself.

Homemade butter caramel is a thing of wonder. Simply boil sugar until it takes on an amber hue, then add cold butter. It bubbles and hisses like a storm inside the pot. Add a touch of flaky salt, and gently swirl until the last bit of butter has been enveloped into the rich caramel sauce. The sauce seems to suddenly appear, with a bit of magic and chemistry. The thing to remember about a true butter caramel is that chemistry is everything. Even the slightest misstep in temperature and it will burn. If even just one sugar crystal drops back into the melted sugar, it will recrystallize before your eyes, nothing to be done about it.

I have a Mauviel copper sauce pot; it's one of my most prized possessions. It's delicate, so you don't want to get it *too* hot. Well, in my haste, I poured the sugar into the pot and went upstairs to finish getting ready, leaving the sugar to heat on the stove. When I returned to smoke filling the kitchen and a black, blobby mess of a pan, I was devastated.

I had ruined my pot. I worked on cleaning that pan for an entire week. I tried every trick. I scraped and scratched with knives to chip away at the thick, black crust burnt to the bottom. I soaked and boiled and finally decided to give up. I drained the pan and went to set it in the garbage. But I just couldn't do it, so I left it on the counter.

A few days went by. One afternoon, I was cleaning the kitchen. As I loaded the dishwasher, I looked at the pot. Was the gunk crackling? I swear if I looked hard, I could see the bottom of the pan. I picked it up and touched the burn; it flaked away as if it were tissue paper. The same burn I had sweated over, scraping and prodding for an entire week to no avail, was flaking away.

"You don't have to try so hard," I whispered under my breath. I kept repeating it to myself again and again. After rubbing it for a short time with my thumb and thumbnail, the black mess finally disappeared to reveal the interior of my unblemished pot.

Sometimes God wants to teach us something. If we'd only let Him work instead of striving and pushing and nearly giving up after the struggle, we'd see He is capable of doing it on His time and in His gentle way. Holding my pot, I quickly thought about my own life at large and how hard I'd been trying to get things done. I thought if I just worked a little harder, everything would be okay. But in reality, in the rest is when the miracle happens.

After the pan dried, the burn literally flaked off with ease. No amount of scraping the wet, burned sugar had helped. Just rest and allow God to work. You'll get to where you are going with much more ease.

Salted Butter Caramel

PREP TIME: *5 minutes* • COOK TIME: *5–10 minutes* • YIELD: *Roughly 12 ounces*

2 cups sugar

3 tablespoons butter

¼ cup heavy cream

Pinch of flaky sea salt

Melt the sugar in a saucepan over medium heat; this takes 5 to 10 minutes and must be done slowly until the sugar is a deep amber color. Turn off the heat. Add the butter and cream; it will sizzle, hiss, and bubble up. Swirl to combine. Add the salt.

The Story of Lydia's Casserole

Sweet and sour meatballs using grape jelly and ground pork? Hot dish? Monster cookies with butter-flavored Crisco? Kielbasa sausages cooked in condensed cream of celery soup and red potatoes? I had never heard of such food until I had the sweetest and most hospitable roommate, Lydia.

You know how every so often, you meet someone who is just the salt of the earth, the kind of person who never gossips and who wears warmth all over them? That was Lydia. Lydia worked in the nursing field, and she was as beautiful as she was gracious. Her family had a pig farm in Ohio, and she taught me so much about life. I, on the other hand, wasn't as kind at this time in my life. I was in my early twenties and more concerned with myself, how I felt, and my own opinions than I was with others. I mean, I always considered myself caring, but I thought I was right about most everything.

Often, when I came home from work, Lydia would be making dinner or cookies or crumbles. She cooked very differently from how I ate growing up, and I loved it. It was true Midwestern comfort food, and she cooked dinner for our little piecemeal family with a real smile.

One evening, I came home starving. Often, Lydia would write her name on her and her boyfriend's lunch, and she'd leave a little container of whatever she'd made for dinner for me. On this particular evening, it was about 11:00 p.m., and I was just praying she'd left me something. Well, she happened to have made my favorite creamy potato and kielbasa sausage casserole. To my dismay, it must have been a small batch because the tiny container I was used to finding for me wasn't there. There was only one container, and it was labeled "Lydia." I stood in the dark kitchen, contemplating by the light of the fridge if I could have just a small bite. She'd never know, I reasoned. *It's so late. Maybe just a tiny bite?*

Who was I? This was not my food! Twenty-two-year-old Danielle did some things I look back on and think, *Wow*. I took a bite; I picked out a hunk of sausage, then another. It took all of three minutes for me to eat all the sausages in her lunch. Panic set in! *What do I do?* I thought. *Do I tell her? Do I eat all the potatoes? Do I run to the store, buy a sausage rope, and attempt to remake it? No, I'll just go to bed and pray to God in Heaven that she doesn't notice.*

The next morning, I received a text message from Lydia.

"Hi Danielle, weird question. Did you eat the sausages out of my lunch?"

Knee-jerk: "No, why?" That was my reaction! *No, why? Danielle*, I thought, *this is very out of character for you. This is terrible. Tell the woman you ate them! She knows!*

I texted, "Maybe it was Mykayla?" We both knew it wasn't Mykayla, our other roommate. She hadn't been home in a week.

Kind, sweet Lydia didn't press it. In fact, she continued to leave me food, and she never stopped making food for me until she moved away about six months later. She bought me a robe and flowers when I lost my job. She made cookies for our neighbors and never asked me about what happened to her lunch after that day.

I didn't realize how powerful an influence on my life Lydia was until years later. Lydia taught me to share, taught me how to love others even when they behave badly or eat all the good parts out of your leftovers. She kept no record of my wrongs, and I am very grateful for her. I didn't talk to Lydia much after she moved away and got married. I heard she moved back to Ohio and has a beautiful family. It's been about fifteen years since the lunch incident, and I think she'd be happy to know I've done some growing in that time.

So there you have it, Lydia. I ate your lunch and lied about it. I'm not sure what got into me, and I'm glad I didn't choose a life of crime, because I don't think I could have made a go of it very well! I know you've forgiven me. Here is a recipe for your glorious, wonderfully creamy sausage and potato bake. I've ditched the canned soup and added a few ingredients. When I make this recipe, I am reminded of the day I ate all the sausage from Lydia's lunch, and in equal measure, I am reminded that grace is very real.

Lydia's Casserole (Creamy Celery, Leek, Potato, and Kielbasa Sausage Bake)

PREP TIME: *20 minutes* • BAKE TIME: *40 minutes* • SERVES: *4–6*

6 medium-sized red potatoes

1 cup finely diced white onion

2 cloves fresh garlic, smashed

2 to 3 tablespoons olive oil

2 tablespoons butter

1½ pounds kielbasa sausage, sliced

4 ribs celery, preferably with
   leaves, sliced on the bias

1 leek, cleaned and sliced

¼ cup all-purpose flour

4 cups chicken stock

2 cups heavy whipping cream

Salt and pepper to taste

1 cup grated parmesan cheese

Parboil the potatoes for 15 minutes in salted water. Drain, cool, and slice into thin rounds.

Preheat the oven to 350°F. Sauté the onion and garlic over medium heat in the olive oil and butter for 2 to 3 minutes. Add the sausage, celery, and leek, and cook for 3 to 4 minutes. Evenly sprinkle the flour over the mixture, and stir to avoid lumps. Cook for another 3 to 4 minutes, then carefully add the stock and cream. Bring to a simmer to thicken. Add the sliced potatoes, and season with salt and pepper. Pour the mixture into a deep, buttered 9-by-13-inch casserole dish. Cover tightly in foil, and bake at least 30 minutes or until the potatoes are tender. Remove the foil and sprinkle with parmesan cheese. Bake uncovered an additional 10 minutes to melt the cheese and crisp the edges of the casserole.

Mixed Greens and Lemony Honey Mustard

PREP TIME: *5 minutes* • CHILL TIME: *2 hours* • MAKES: *1 cup*

½ cup mayonnaise

1½ tablespoons yellow mustard

1 tablespoon spicy brown mustard

1 tablespoon honey

1 teaspoon dried chives or 1
    tablespoon fresh chives

½ teaspoon cracked black pepper

¼ teaspoon garlic powder

¼ teaspoon onion powder

Juice of 1 lemon

Kosher salt to taste

4 to 6 cups mixed greens

Combine all the ingredients except mixed greens, and refrigerate 2 hours and up to overnight before serving. Serve dressing with your favorite mixed greens. This dressing is best made the day before and will last one week in the refrigerator.

Cherry Heaven

When Noah was a baby, I managed to book a side job doing makeup for some models on a local television segment. Often on the local news, there would be a paid ad for a department store talking about spring trends. The department stores I worked for always asked the counter artists if they would be available to provide the models with makeup before going on air. I always wanted to do it. When I finally got chosen, I was over-the-moon excited!

I felt like this was my big break. I couldn't believe that I was going to do makeup for a television segment on the local news! The day came for me to head up to Seattle and meet the models I'd be working on. But Noah had had a very sleepless night, developed a fever, and was too sick for me to work that day.

I was so sad. I felt like I was *supposed* to do that job. My baby came first though, and I called out sick. My team wasn't very happy with me, and I was never asked to apply for the segments again. At the time, I remember thinking, *Well, that's it. There goes my big break in the makeup world.* Missing that opportunity was something I thought about a lot that year. I figured that if I couldn't make it in the restaurant biz, I *should* be making it in the makeup world.

Sometimes we must let everything go in order to grow. It is possible to let something go while still working or moving in an area of your life. Letting go for me meant not striving. When I called out on that job, I let go of the need to *be something*. I continued to work in makeup, growing and healing without even being aware of the massive work being done in my heart. I started focusing on taking one step forward gratefully instead of taking on the world. And that approach gave me some peace.

That year, Mike and I began to slowly work on our first cookbook. I didn't have end goals beyond finishing it and getting it out in the world somehow. I didn't have any grand ideas of television or large-scale success. I just knew in my core that I had to move in the direction of writing a book, trusting in the Lord along the way. Just being able to preserve the recipes we made at Minoela was so essential to healing my heart.

When we finally self-published in 2014, it felt like a massive accomplishment. And we needed to promote the book if I wanted to get it into people's hands. Around that time, I saw a few cooking segments on local television shows, writers and cooks and creators promoting books, projects, and gadgets. I was reminded of the TV segment I'd had to miss out on a few years before. I was hard at work doing makeup and freelance food styling for a couple of regional magazines as my book had its debut. I found an email address from my makeup segment a couple of years before and sent a letter to a producer. I explained who I was and how I'd love to promote my book.

I never heard back. Six months went by, and a fellow makeup artist I worked with said to me, "You should go do that local show! Show 'em your book!"

"Hey, if you know anyone, help a girl out!" I told her.

It turned out she did know somebody. She sent an email off, and we both hoped for the best. More time passed. Then late one evening, I received an email from a producer on the show. She wrote, "Hi, Danielle. We've had a last-minute cancellation, and I was wondering if you would make something on air from the cover of *South Sound Magazine!*"

I couldn't believe it! I had styled a ramen noodle dish that Mike had photographed and that had recently been published on the cover of *South Sound*. The cover had caught the producer's eye right around the time my coworker's email reached her! Could this be happening?

We started a back-and-forth about the details of the segment. There was no budget, they informed me, so I would have to purchase the ingredients and bring them to the show myself. Of course, I had to do it!

When I got to the station, they led me to a back room where I could prepare. I cooked up the food and met with my producer. She was a kind, small woman with blond hair and a big grin. She walked me through everything. I met the show's host and sat before the tiny studio audience. There were just a few cameras and lights, and I felt so special. I wondered how many people would make this dish after seeing it on TV. I hoped I wouldn't mess up. I brought my cooking pans from home. They were pretty beat up but well loved. I made my ramen and did the best I could. The segment flowed nicely, the host and I had a warm rapport, and I didn't burn anything!

When I went offstage, the producer came up to me. She said, "Danielle, that was great! I didn't know you'd done television before."

I said, "Me? No, I've never done TV before. This was my big debut. Well, I was on the *Ranger Charlie & Rosco* when I was about ten, but that probably doesn't count." We both laughed.

"You are a natural," she said. "You can't teach what you have on camera."

I just stood there and drank in her words. *Me? I'm a natural on camera?*

She went on to say that perhaps we should plan more segments. "I'd love to do something monthly with you. Send me some ideas!"

I cleaned up my things and couldn't stop thinking about what she said. *You are a natural. You can't teach what you have.* Our words hold weight. They can be used for good if we let them. Her words sparked a new path for me. Up to that point, I'd never seriously considered pursuing a career in television. Growing up, I had done some auditions for *Star Search* and *Survivor*. I'd even had a few acting auditions for traveling casting agents while in high school. But I had never been cast in any productions.

I didn't know how I'd pursue television, but I took her words and tucked them into my soul. I appeared for dozens of segments on that little local show. I cut my teeth doing cooking demos, getting increasingly more comfortable on camera. I'd pack up my wagon of supplies, drop Noah off with a babysitter, and head on over to the station before my makeup shift began.

Following my third or fourth appearance, I asked the producer if she knew the producers of any other regional programs. Maybe Portland or California? I told her I'd love to teach a cooking demo on another show. But little did I know, my questions sort of broke protocol. There's a taboo in the television industry whereby it's seen as terribly rude to ask for access to appear on a show other than the one you are currently appearing on. I later discovered it's something that you just don't do. In hindsight, it makes sense, but I was merely eager to set big things in motion.

She said, "Oh, gosh. I'll think about it, but I don't think I know anyone."

I didn't pay it much mind and took her at her word. As the months went on, we grew to be very friendly with each other. She pulled me aside one morning as I prepared my food for a segment.

By now, we were six months down the road and into our eighth or ninth segment together. She said, "Danielle, remember when I told you I didn't know anyone in television? Well, turns out I do. I have some friends in New York City. I am going to reach out. I think you guys would have a lot of fun."

I was thrilled. "Wait," I said. "I thought you didn't know anyone!"

She grinned slyly. "I didn't know how much I was going to like you," she said. "You need to be seen. As soon as you start doing national shows, buckle up! You are going to get scooped up!"

She put me in contact with the executive producer at a major national television show. It took some time, but the woman agreed to chat with me after several emails back and forth. I sent her many potential segment possibilities, and every time she replied kindly, but I hadn't yet received an invitation onto the show. I'd tell her about my books and share my philosophies on cooking and life and how the two intertwine. I would forward her clips of my local television appearances. She began thanking me for getting in touch. "I appreciate you sending your latest segment. It's great! If you are ever in NYC, let me know." We had been emailing for months at this point. I had to get to NYC!

In the wake of our work on our first book, Mike and I had begun teaching workshops and sharing our method for how to shoot food. The workshops were beautiful. I styled the food and Michael took the photos, and by this time, folks were flying from all over the country to participate in our humble classes.

It felt surreal. I was doing local television, and we both had full-time jobs and this little side hustle called Rustic Joyful Food. I had a message I needed people to hear: *Life is good today, no matter what.*

I had an idea! We'd host a workshop in New York City! Mike was skeptical. "We have never been to New York. How do we teach there?" he asked.

"I'll figure it out," I said. "I promise!"

Well, I reached out to that executive producer and explained that I'd be teaching in New York, and I'd love to be on the show! Still no booking. But I didn't stop. I found a studio space in Brooklyn that would cost $4,000 for the day. How could I pay that? I had to choose one that was impressive enough and large enough for the number of attendees I would need to pay for it all. The math revealed I would need about $10,000 to cover travel, the rentals, food, and a hotel room for the week. How would I pull that off? This workshop had to be stunning, had to put every other workshop we'd ever done to shame.

I asked the studio to give me a bit of time to come up with the deposit. I advertised the workshop: $1,000 per ticket. And we sold four on the first day. This was happening! We were going to New York. I started inviting prominent food editors and some prolific food industry people in hopes that they might join us.

I sent off yet another email asking to meet the executive of the show I was trying to book. I explained the workshop and how if I couldn't get booked, then maybe we could at least meet. I prayed and crossed my fingers. She agreed! This was incredible. One step closer. When the time came, I packed a suitcase full of my most prized styling props, said a prayer, and off we flew.

Most of that meeting was a blur of nerves and overtalking on my part. We met up with some of their culinary team so that they might ask me a few cooking-related questions. We chatted all of ten minutes. She asked me thoughtfully why I thought I was different and what I had to offer in a very saturated culinary world. I paused, and the only thing I could think to say was that I was just me. I was always going to be just myself. No gimmicks, no shtick. Myself was the only thing I knew how to be, and I was only ever going to be this girl. Added to the fact that I was a damn good cook, and well, it just worked. If someone asks what you have to offer, always feel proud to say that you bring something to the table just by walking in the gifts God has naturally given you. You are an asset, and you don't need a gimmick.

Months later, that meeting worked out. I began appearing on that show doing cooking segments.

I learned things about myself in New York. I had this fire in me, the longest burning fire I'd ever had. Something wouldn't let it go. There was this purpose I couldn't deny, and I came to realize that everything I had been through, every loss and tear, was stored up for this moment in Manhattan.

Everything that has happened in your life happened to deliver you to this very moment. If we'd just lean into the storms knowing the wake after will grow our hearts and define our steps and inform our choices, we'd be braver. It's so valuable to never lose sight of that; we are right where we need to be.

After my meeting with that producer in New York, I stood on the corner when I got back out onto the street. I called my mom and told her I thought the meeting went great. I was still a bundle of nerves, but I thought I did well. She said, "Don't forget Cherry Heaven, Dan."

Cherry Heaven was our name for a field near our house growing up where we'd go in the summer to pick cherries, forage, and play. It was a place where my siblings and I had lovely childhood adventures in uncharted territory. It was a place we loved, where we enjoyed life, where we explored, where life was profoundly simply and small in the best way.

Don't forget where you came from. When I was young, my mom often took us out for drives. We didn't always know where she was headed; I'm not sure she even knew. But she always found trees for us to climb and fruit to pick, and Cherry Heaven was one of the unexpected places we discovered. We were celebration in motion, loving and living and soaking in the glory of our childhoods. I hadn't forgotten Cherry Heaven and how it found us at just the right time. We went exploring and found Cherry Heaven. Sometimes we have to set out on that drive with no destination in sight in order to discover our path. We won't find it sitting at home or crying over loss. We must find it by doing things that may scare us. I was very afraid to host that workshop in Brooklyn. But if I hadn't forged ahead, I wouldn't be on this path. Uncharted territory brings hardships but great rewards.

We don't know what life holds, but we must set out and explore. We must venture out, even if we are scared. God gave us hopes and dreams and skills that we must act on. Big, good things happen when we are true to ourselves and honor the fire he placed in our souls.

He Is Merciful

It turns out I don't have very smooth pregnancies. They are an exercise in survival and careful consideration of my every move. They are, however, worth every moment of bed rest and every sleepless night because the end reward is unmatched.

When I found out we were expecting Milo, I remember walking down the hallway of our apartment and telling Noah first, "Our family is going to have a baby!"

Noah immediately began to cry and jump for joy, and he said something I'll never forget. He said, "Oh, Mama, I prayed for this baby!" He was all of five years old and so precious.

"Me too, darling," I said. "Me too."

I've often felt that the thing we want the most, that thing we pray for, can sometimes, in its realization, bring us to our knees in hardship and severe difficulty. Early in my pregnancy with Noah, I discovered I had placenta previa, which led to severe bleeding, which led to strict bed rest. And once again, pregnant with Milo, I became ill. The bleeding began, and it was an all-out war for my body to keep Milo. I had gestational diabetes and lost a great deal of weight during the pregnancy. I was once again on bed rest, and loneliness set in. Just as with my first pregnancy and bed rest, my side work began to dry up a bit. Just prior to getting pregnant, Mike and I felt like we were on the cusp of a breakthrough in our business. But with all the medical issues I was having, I'd have to set our business aside for a year. Many of my friendships dwindled. I looked fine on the outside, but I had to stay in bed. I couldn't make it out much for dinners or parties. I was perpetually winded and exhausted. I was testing my blood sugar nine times a day and injecting myself with insulin, and the injections left big, black bruises all over my stomach. I'd cry because I felt like no one really understood what I was going through. Mike was gone all day and most of the nights, working; he headed out around 2:00 a.m. and didn't make it home some days until three or four in the afternoon. It was just me and my five-year-old, a little boy who needed a lot of activity, to run and jump and play. But I couldn't do any of those things with him. Guilt crept in. I wasn't cleaning my house. No one was coming to help me. I desperately wanted someone to come save me and take care of me. Why was I so lonely and sick? I was scared I would lose the baby. I questioned everything.

God allows lonely seasons. He allows broken seasons. He allows seasons that seem like four winters in a row. But these seasons aren't punishment; they are sanctified. They are meant to draw us near to Him. They are meant to teach us that no matter what, He is for us. We almost never recognize this in the middle of the season, however. For me, it generally comes afterward. This pregnancy was a trial, and I limped along spiritually and physically. What was God doing? I'd think, *I thought we were on a path, Lord? I thought we were done with hard times.*

To walk with Jesus isn't a guarantee that life will be easy. I'd rationalized that hard times in my life meant I'd done something wrong. With Minoela, I thought I could see how selfish I'd been, and I could understand why we'd lost our home and restaurant. I had been self-absorbed and uncaring toward my husband, and I felt that I deserved the losses. But that belief couldn't have been further from the truth. The truth is that I opened a restaurant, and because I was young and inexperienced in all the ways that mattered, it failed. But I learned so much from running Minoela. God used Minoela to shape me, not to punish me. We make choices in life. Sometimes those choices yield total financial success, and sometimes you lose your house and car. But even then, God is working behind the scenes for your greater purpose.

And then, after five years of praying, here comes another baby! I wasn't being punished through these trials. I was being blessed with a beautiful child. I needed to understand that God isn't mad at me when hard things happen. Sometimes we fall ill, lose loved ones, or even lose a child, but we did nothing wrong. These are experiences that happen because we are human. They tear us apart. But we are never alone. As long as there is breath in our lungs, we can cling to Jesus. He loves us more than we could ever fathom. Life isn't always fair and peachy, and one person may birth five kids in a row without issue while another woman deals with persistent infertility. This doesn't mean God loves one woman more. He loves each one equally, and He is using their journey for His glory to be shown in their lives. Not for *our* glory. For *His* glory, so that we might share our experience and encourage someone else in the storm.

God isn't mad at you. I used to think He was angry with me, but I know now that I couldn't have been more wrong. In the case of my pregnancies, He was blessing my family with children who'd change everything I understood about mercy and grace.

With Milo, my water broke at twenty-nine weeks and six days, and I checked into the hospital where I had delivered Noah. Every meal was brought to me, and I was terrified but also at peace. For over two weeks, we kept the baby inside to continue growing. Noah went to stay with my parents, and Mike continued working, heading to the hospital as soon as he was off every day. Those few weeks were intense. The baby could have come at any moment, but every hour in the womb was precious.

My sister would visit me and then my parents. And then Mike would arrive. In the hospital cafeteria, they discovered the Jazz Bar, a cream cheese lemon bar that was beyond delightful. It was this tiny shortbread crust triangle with blueberries in it and creamy, tart lemon filling. They snuck one to me every single day. This little lemon bar was a bright spot in a hard time. People say hospital food is terrible, but I found it wonderful not having to cook for myself. The BLT was a treat, and the salmon and broccoli were just as good as at any restaurant. I know these little things were just gifts to get me through. My situation was delicate and potentially dangerous to the baby, and if I had lain there dwelling on it, I would have had no peace. Instead, I wrote lists, prayed, slept, and looked forward to my daily Jazz Bar delivery and salmon dinner. To this day, Milo loves salmon, mashed potatoes, and broccoli more than any other food, and I attribute it to my diet in those weeks just prior to his birth.

We hadn't yet settled on a name for our little guy. For most of the pregnancy, Mike and I thought his name was Wilder. We loved that name, but deep in my heart, I knew it wasn't *his* name. I prayed to discover what his true name would be, but nothing came. The day before he was born, I was googling boy names and came upon Milo. I hadn't heard this name in ages. It was so soft and sweet. It reminded me of everything I'd risked for my baby. A gentle spirit. An abundant life. Name meanings are almost more important than the actual name for me. Milo means merciful. Oh, how merciful I was coming to find the Lord had been to me. He was caring delicately for me. I had good doctors, and our bills were paid. My husband had a good job. And I wasn't being punished—I was completely taken care of.

Those few weeks in the hospital revealed God's intention for my life. He never intended to leave my side. He intended to bless our family with another baby, and He intended to continue to heal my marriage and prosper our business.

I have heard many people say that a business can't thrive unless you pour everything into it. Just eat, sleep, and breathe your calling or passion. Not true! God can cause you to have wonderful ideas, and He can favor you and cause the right opportunities to come along, opportunities that have nothing to do with your performance. My good deeds didn't get me anywhere in life; God did. I was understanding His heart more than I ever had before, and even in the detail of naming Milo, I was experiencing His mercies over not only my life but Mike's and Noah's lives. We were right where we were supposed to be, fully cared for, fully accepted. Just walking a hard road with a merciful God. Not an angry God waiting to punish me for my transgressions but one filled with love and care for every detail.

When you are on hospital bed rest with broken water, the stress of both baby and mama are carefully monitored, and if at any time either are in distress, it's *go time*. We hit our go time, and I knew something wasn't quite right in my body. Milo's heart rate had dropped enough that the doctor felt it was time for an emergency C-section. A team of nurses came into my room at a moment's notice and began prepping me for what would be a very difficult experience. Mike was wearing scrubs and ready to accompany me, but he was told he wouldn't be able to due to the emergency nature of the situation. And just like that, I was inside the OR, and things felt rushed and chaotic. But I was not afraid.

I received my epidural, but I had adrenaline pumping through my body, and Milo's heart rate continued to drop quickly. My doctor began the C-section, and I could feel it. She said, "Can we feel that, Danielle?"

I said, "Yes, ma'am, I can!"

She called back to the anesthesiologist, "Put her out!"

"I'll need an assist!" he said.

She yelled back, in the most commanding voice, "NOW!"

Then a nurse put the anesthesia mask over my mouth and nose. I felt like I was at war, and this was my time for battle. I knew that we were in for it, and I prayed as things went dark.

When I woke up, I couldn't open my eyes because of the anesthesia. I was back in my room, surrounded by a team of doctors and my family. Crying, I yelled out, "Is he okay?" One of the doctors confirmed that he was out and okay. "His name is Milo!" I shouted, declaring God's mercy over this baby.

What I didn't know in that moment was what had taken place while I was unconscious. They pulled Milo out of me, and he wasn't breathing. They announced a code blue over the hospital's loudspeaker, and all hands were on deck. In my room, my mom, sister, and Mike, anxious and waiting, were alerted to the baby's condition as things progressed. The medical team had difficulty setting a breathing tube in Milo, so they called the head of neonatology, who was at home, and he arrived at the OR inside fifteen minutes. He set the tube on his second try. Milo didn't receive oxygen for fifteen minutes after birth. They told my family they didn't know if he'd make it through the night.

When I awoke and began proclaiming that the baby's name was Milo, nobody immediately told me how serious the situation was. They took me to recover and said he was beautiful. And strong. They said he was alive.

After some rest and recovery, of course they brought me up to speed on his condition. He was being treated in the neonatal infant care unit. I didn't get to hold him for three days. I couldn't walk well due to my fast and wild C-section, and I wasn't recovering very well. I stayed in the hospital for six days after Milo's birth. I was able to visit his NICU incubator isolette in a wheelchair. He weighed only three pounds. They assured me he was progressing beautifully, better than expected. He would have a tough road ahead of him, but he was alive.

One of the darling NICU nurses read me his birth report. I was not aware that they give a test score upon birth, but it's called an Apgar score, and it's used to check a baby's heart rate, muscles, and other signs to see if additional specialized or emergency care is needed. Milo was given a 0, indicating he had little to no chance of survival. The test doesn't necessarily indicate long-term medical problems, but it highlights what the infant's needs are upon being born.

Here he was, one of the sickest babies in the NICU, but he was making tiny improvements. God was so merciful to us in saving Milo.

The hospital was over fifty miles away from where we lived. I needed to be with my baby, but I wasn't healing well. Even after I went home, I was sweating and throwing up, and I could tell something was wrong. I attributed my condition to all we'd been through. Weeks of bed rest plus exhaustion from driving back and forth to hold my delicate baby, who was connected to breathing machines, feeding tubes, and monitors—of course my body wasn't working perfectly. None of this was normal, but I was grateful Milo was even here in the world, so I pushed on as best I could.

One morning about ten days after this, I felt very strange, panicky, my heart racing. I wasn't eating very much, and all I thought about was getting back to see Milo. I called for Mike and told him it felt like I was dying. He said, "Oh no, babe, let's get you in the shower to cool off."

The last thing I remember was telling Mike to call 911. I was going into septic shock. It turned out broken water, slow healing, and a rip-roaring, rough-and-tumble cesarean section created a prime condition for infection to start. I'd had a fever for days that I'd been keeping at bay with medicine. The infection began to spread. I'd never heard the word *sepsis* before, but I had it.

I was in the ICU for six days, in a different hospital than where Milo was being treated. During this time, I prayed and cried and clung to God's promises. I felt like a failure. I asked God for my life, for Him to heal my body.

And heal my body He did. It took a long time, but He absolutely did. The last night I spent in the ICU, I felt strongly convicted that it was time to complete our next cookbook, a project we had begun but then set aside given the circumstances of my pregnancy. Given all the more pressing issues at hand, I immediately thought, *What, Lord? Now?*

How was I supposed to write a book? With what money? With what resources? I was so sick. My baby was still in the NICU and would stay there for another month. But all the internal questioning led me to speak to Mike about it. He came into my room at the hospital, and I said, "I think we are supposed to finish *Generations*."

He smiled and said, "Now?"

I said, "Yes, I think now. It's time."

He said, "Okay!" One of Mike's best qualities is that he isn't a dream squasher. He is a big champion. He said, "I don't know when we are going to have the time, but if it's what you'd like to do, let's do it."

As my body healed, we made daily visits to Milo in the NICU. When we brought him home, he was just over four pounds. He was a happy and peaceful baby. He had a tracheal condition that labored his breathing, so I held him through the night in my lap. I'd have my phone in one hand or my laptop at the kitchen table, and I'd write. I'd write to heal my heart. I'd write to remember my childhood. I'd write to calm my fears, and I'd write because the Lord gently nudged me in that direction. Each time I've written a book, the Lord has done such a work in healing my heart through the process that I'm convinced the action of writing recipes and telling stories is my therapy.

Writing *Generations* helped me navigate postpartum life. I was deeply affected by all that had gone on. Some days, it was hard to care for Milo, and I needed time to heal. There seems to be a common opinion that we are supposed to feel a certain way after having a baby and that if we don't, we get disconnected from our child. Don't box yourself into thinking it's supposed to be a certain way. Holding Milo and writing until midnight helped me care for him. It eased me into mothering this precious boy whose first months were so terrifying. I worked through a lot of trauma with Milo, and he is a true picture of God's mercies. Writing through the night saved me.

We went on to self-publish *Generations*, and by Christmas of that year, we had a book in the world. We crowdfunded just as we had with our first cookbook, and we did the photography under our living room window. Creating the book was a peaceful, healing experience. God's mercies were never more evident to me than they were during that time.

If I could make sure you knew one thing deep in your soul, it'd be that *God isn't mad at you.* Just the opposite—He delights in you! He desires good for you. That doesn't mean it's going to be easy as a Christian, but it does mean He won't ever leave your side. He will show up in a merciful way. He will bring you bright spots in dark times: lemon bars by way of a friend, a full tank of gas when you have no money, and any other number of small blessings. Maybe a special note from a loved one. Or even the act of writing.

Milo's first two years were not what might be called "normal."

There were endless doctor's visits, developmental delays, and other challenges resulting from his prematurity. But as of this writing, he has caught up beautifully, and he is healthy, happy, and on track for a wonderful childhood.

Mike and I were talking the other day about how we experience God. We all see and feel God in our lives in different ways. For Mike, he sees the power of the Holy Spirit at work in poetry, and I see Him in nature and cooking. Who knew I'd count a cream cheese lemon bar as a mercy of the Lord? But I will take it! God knows just how to speak to us. He created us. My prayer for you this moment is for you to feel His mercies and see Him at work in your life even if it doesn't immediately feel like He's there. He's in it with you, and He will never leave you.

Aunty Charlotte

Some pains in life can't be explained. There is simply no explanation for our sufferings or our disappointments or the hands we've been dealt that we had absolutely no control of. We want to believe if we just work harder or eat a better diet, we are the captains of our own destiny. Surely we can work hard enough to heal it or fix it. But what happens when the healing doesn't come? Is God still sovereign? Does He still care so deeply and tenderly for us? I believe the answer is yes. I believe that there may be some things in our lives that no amount of explaining will ever resolve. But I also know that the heart of our savior is for us, during every battle and every loss. We live in a fallen world, riddled with sin. We get caught in the crosshairs of other people's poor choices, leaving us with broken childhoods and broken hearts. I believe God is still near. He, being close to us, can offer respite during times we will never have answers. To cry out to Jesus is medicine for a weary and broken soul. I believe that He can work all our tragedy for His glory to be shown in our lives. Not fancy glory but healing glory. I believe He can speak peace into a situation that doesn't have any answer and makes no sense. It takes time, it takes faith, and it is not easy. There may never be a full understanding of sickness or disease, and when healing doesn't come, I must choose to believe that He knows. Only He can give full peace and restoration in our hearts and minds when we trust Jesus with all of us, not just the things that feel good. I think of this often when I think of my aunty Charlotte.

Some of my earliest memories involve a beautiful, kidney-shaped, deep-indigo swimming pool and buckets of fried chicken. Potato salad with dill pickle relish *only* and lawn chairs strewn about an oasis of beautiful plants and flowers. I never liked plants much as a kid, but I'd follow Aunty Charlotte around her and Uncle Bill's yard as she pointed out every newly planted bloom or foliage. I'd never seen a strawberry planter until Aunty Charlotte showed me one. Little dips and spouts protruded from a terra-cotta urn for tucking strawberry plants into. I remember warm sunlight on my shoulders as I swam in her pool. You couldn't keep me out of the water. Every summer, we'd go back, until we didn't.

Growing older is hard. You never know it's the last time you'll ever do something until it's the last time.

My aunty Charlotte is warm and kind, with salt-and-pepper hair and soft, almond eyes. She playfully says, "Oh, Billy, stop that!" to Uncle Bill and always greets you with such a big smile. As a child, I'd sneak upstairs at the big family reunions and grab an extra fried chicken leg, eating it and just wandering around the property.

It's nice to be a child. No small talk is ever required. I think this time is when I learned to love stealing away at a party. To this day, I'll find a corner or an empty room to be alone in while the other partygoers enjoy.

The last time I visited Aunty Charlotte's home, no one told me it'd be the last time. This was just after Noah was born. Aunty Charlotte still remembered then.

Long gone were the days when I'd steal away until the sun went down and it was time to drive home. My family would take one last tour of the yard before a teary Uncle Bill and Aunty Charlotte would see us off, waving as the blue hour slipped into nighttime. Always in July, always around 9:30.

That would be the last time I'd ever visit Aunty Charlotte and Uncle Bill's home, the last time I'd enjoy a bucket of fried chicken with extra pickles. By this point, it'd been a few years since Great Gran passed away, and with her went the regular summer reunions at that Gresham, Oregon, home. Sometimes, what I wouldn't give to go back to the eighth grade when the only thing I seemed to worry about was what I'd be when I grew up.

Well, now I *am* all grown up, and my aunty Charlotte has

slipped away. She's still here, earth side. Dementia may have robbed her of her mind, but I know that our savior holds her heart. He is still tenderly caring for her soul until it's time for her to take her last breath. There is still so much joy in her life. She still admires the plants and foliage and life. She loves sweets and slow strolls.

As for the home I'd steal away to every summer of my childhood? I may never be there again. I think that forgiveness and time mend broken bridges and shore up periods of pain in our lives. It's hard to think of people we love no longer as they were. I've forgiven the cruel part of this life that leaves us feeling broken and missing family we no longer get to see anymore. God has given us beautiful memories. I will always remember the beauty. I'll always remember fried chicken and strawberry planters and walking the yard to look at the plants. I find a lot of peace these days in growing, in warm sun, in dirt on my hands. I love to grow a garden and watch the transformation that occurs there, to plant and witness growth, fruitfulness, dying, and new, fresh life the following year.

I know Aunty Charlotte is still in there somewhere. I imagine that the tiny memory connectors suffer a break somehow and can no longer connect. Trauma, and a line breaks. Bitterness, and a line breaks. Simply living sometimes might break the lines.

From now until forever, I'll tend to tiny strawberry plants and remember to cherish each day, each breath, and to write down every memory. I'll read them aloud when memory fails and time has stolen away the once-vibrant rituals, like walking the yard to view the plants or swimming in that pool.

I think that my love of plants and growing things came from Aunty Charlotte. I'd sit on the railroad ties as a child in my mother's garden, watching bees land on zinnias and picking snap peas and raspberries straight off the plant as my polyester Rainbow Brite nightgown swept along in the dirt and low-hanging leaves. This love for the garden is deep in my soul. It urges me to lovingly remember, and it helps me to heal. Terra-cotta strawberry planters always serve as a fond reminder of the past. I will forever be grateful for the women who were giants in my life, women who went before me, formed me, and gave me purpose. I'll continue to give my unexplained grief and loss over to the one who keeps my heart. I'll remember the good stuff. And just as my darling aunty Charlotte would want, from now until forever, to the strawberries and the garden I will tend.

Old-Fashioned Dill Potato Salad

PREP TIME: *10 minutes* • COOK TIME: *20 minutes* • CHILL TIME: *2–4 hours* •
YIELD: *4–6 servings*

5 white or gold potatoes, peeled

6 eggs, room temperature

1 cup diced dill pickle

1 cup mayonnaise

½ cup chopped fresh dill

½ cup yellow mustard

¼ cup pickle juice (from the jar)

1 rib celery, diced

¼ white onion, grated

Cover the potatoes with water in a large pot, and bring to a boil. Reduce heat to maintain a slow boil, and cook for 10 minutes. Add the eggs, and cook for another 10 minutes; this will allow for everything to finish cooking at the same time. Drain, cool, peel the eggs, then dice the potatoes and eggs, and place in a large mixing bowl. Add the remaining ingredients, mix gently, and taste for salt and pepper. Refrigerate 2 to 4 hours before serving.

Strawberry Lemonade

PREP TIME: *15 minutes* • YIELD: *Roughly 1½ quarts*

4 to 5 lemons

1 cup fresh strawberries, smashed

1½ cups sugar

4 to 6 cups water, depending on taste

Squeeze the lemons into a large pitcher (this should yield about 1 cup), and add the strawberries and sugar. Stir to incorporate, and allow to sit for about 10 minutes or until the sugar granules have completely dissolved. Add the water, then add additional water to suit your own lemonade tastes. Serve over ice.

Pineapple Mint

I love mint growing in a garden. There is something peaceful and delightful about it. It's calming to see mint blanketing pathways and gardens. Many years ago, a friend told me you can plant mint anywhere. She had beautiful pineapple mint plants in her garden. I'd never seen or heard of pineapple mint before. It's almost fluffy, and each of the leaves has a white border. The leaves are soft. When you pick it, you most definitely get the sweet mint aroma, along with an underlying, intoxicating tropical fragrance.

My friend's garden had beautiful plumes of pineapple mint all over. She told me that at any time I wanted, I could clip some of her mint, tuck it into an area of my garden, and a few weeks later, I'd have my own plants. This fascinated me! How delight-ful. And in just a few weeks!

After we moved to Issaquah, I was trying to make a home in a place that didn't feel like home. I found out I could rent a little garden plot each season in our apartment complex, and I did so. I walked the garden and discovered pineapple mint in several of the plots. I remembered what my friend told me years before: "This little guy will flourish in a few weeks' time. That's how hearty mint is. Wherever you plant it, it will grow." I clipped three or four sprigs and planted them in my plot.

By the next day, they had withered fully. A week later, they were just husks. I kept watering them, but nothing happened. That garden season came to a close, and I was a little sad the mint never took root.

Noah was two years old and loved to be in the garden with me, so we spent a lot of time there through that fall and into winter. Nothing grew very well for us during this season. It was my first year away from the region where I'd grown up, and I wanted des-perately to cultivate a beautiful garden in this new place to pro-vide a bit of a reprieve from everything else going on in my life. I thought to myself, *Of course my mint didn't grow*. It was perhaps just my luck. My luck wasn't so good, I used to think. I thought of the mint that wouldn't grow often that winter, and it reminded me of my failures and that I missed my home and the life I knew.

Winter came and went, and spring arrived once again. I thought I'd try to plant a real spring garden: lettuces and radishes and peas. The peas never came up. I must have laid sixty seeds in rows to make sure I could thin them properly. Not a single sprout. The radishes came up and tasted horrible. Maybe gardening just wasn't for me.

Summer arrived, and I spent time weeding and preparing for tomatoes. I bought some rosemary and sage plants. I marched out to plant them, and there in the corner of my plot, I noticed dozens of tiny, soft sprouts with white-edged leaves. *No, it couldn't be,* I thought.

The pineapple mint! Sure enough, there she was. Beneath the ground, she had been developing roots. What I had believed to be long gone and dried up was actually beginning to thrive. My pineapple mint was the pure representation of perfect timing.

Sometimes in life, things—relationships, businesses, hopes and dreams—may seem broken and gone, as though they've died. We try our best, and just when it seems these things won't thrive, they spring forth full of life at the very moment we need them to. That first year in Issaquah, it felt like my garden had failed. But beneath the surface, God was working. He was moving on my behalf. Those first mint cuttings turned into dozens of sprouts. They flourished in my tiny apartment garden plot. In the end, they were the only thing that grew prolifically in my garden. It was a stunning reminder that though we might seem done, empty, or washed up and in a new place, after a period of rest and healing, we can come back far better and stronger for it in the end.

I'd clip the mint and steep it in boiling water with honey and lemon season after season during our time in Issaquah. The leaves would swirl about my clear glass tumbler as I poured the boiling water over top. I'd sit in my chair at the front window, thinking about my new life. It was a good life, and I was thriving even if it didn't always feel like it. Just as the mint had thrived.

I count the five years we lived in that apartment as the most difficult and beautiful of my life. You may be struggling and feel as though you might be withering. But know that below the soil, you are putting down roots that are strong enough to hold you up. When I see beautiful plumes of unique, precious pineapple mint, I am reminded of how God used the flourishing mint in my plot to show me my own resilience.

She's hearty, you see. You can plant her anywhere, and she'll thrive.

Pineapple Mint Tea

PREP TIME: *5–10 minutes* • YIELD: *12 ounces*

½ cup packed fresh pineapple mint
   leaves (or any other mint variety)

2 cups boiling water

Lemon slices

Honey (optional)

Splash of cream (optional)

Place the mint in a tall 12-ounce heatproof glass tumbler or mug. Pour boiling water on top. Allow the mint to steep 3 to 5 minutes, depending on how strong you prefer your tea. Garnish with lemon, and add honey and cream if desired.

New Shoes

In the past few years, I've been taking big leaps in growth in my life. Big setbacks and big leaps forward. And some of it, believe it or not, had to do with shoes.

I had this trusty old pair of tennis shoes I liked to travel in. I'd made a habit of faithfully bleaching the soles before I traveled, then running them through the washing machine so they'd look as good as new, or at least a step closer to new. I loved them dearly. I was traveling monthly between cities for work, and these shoes were my traveling companions. It's hard for me to find comfy shoes I love, shoes that make my feet look nice. So I'd faithfully clean and wash my old worn shoes to wear for every work trip, even though they really should have been reserved only for mowing the lawn.

I'd been exploring my own style more and more as I did TV segments. I loved wearing button-down shirts and white jeans with my clean, fresh kicks. I went out shopping and happened upon some adorable new Adidas tennis shoes. These shoes had that nineties clamshell toe and rose-gold stripes. I'd only ever owned the knockoffs in junior high, and for some reason, these babies were back in style. My thirty-six-year-old self was screaming with excitement for the thirteen-year-old me from decades past. It felt good to wear new tennis shoes that were so cozy and light and also to feel young and stylish. I'd get to set, swap out my outfit, and take off my old shoes to put on my new shoes for the show. As soon as we'd finish, I'd slip them off and carefully tuck them away into my bag, then slide my old tennis shoes on. I was always mildly embarrassed about wearing the old ones, but they were reliable, they were practical, and why would I ever wear fresh, gleaming white shoes to the airport? I wanted to keep my new shoes new!

One day in LA, I finished up my work and was preparing to catch my Uber to the airport. I had changed my clothes and was wearing my old shoes. For some reason, I sat down in the trailer with the new shoes on my lap and the old shoes on my feet. At that moment, I wondered how I was ever going to go to the places I dreamed of if I kept putting the old shoes on. Even after I was able to afford new shoes, I'd put my old ones on to feel safe. I mean, I'd reason with myself, *Don't get the new ones dirty. Stick with the old ones. I might get a blister!* The Adidas were new after all, and I'd better not walk too far in them. Old is best.

Sometimes when we learn better, we learn *to do* better. It's hard to adopt the better way, because old habits and views die hard. It's easy to slip back into old ways, to gussy up the old shoes because they feel safe. It's tough to walk in new shoes, because it's uncomfortable for a time. When God reaches into our hearts and changes our perspective, we aren't supposed to want the old any longer. But it's sure easy to slip back into old habits.

I sat there with my new shoes on my lap. This great metaphor for my life was unfolding. For so long, I'd been striving, pushing, slipping on my old shoes even after God showed me a better way. I took my old tennis shoes off and tucked them into the trailer's garbage can. I put my new shoes on, picked up my suitcase, and opened the door. You see, sometimes where you are going, the old ways just won't do. The old thoughts and old relationships and old routines simply won't hold up to the amazing things God is doing in your life. I turned to take one last look at that old pair of shoes, grateful for every step I took in them and for everything I learned during the three years we walked together. Then I turned around and, with tears in my eyes, marched forward, possibility of blisters and all.

Brand-new is scary and unknown, but that kind of growth requires fully leaning on Jesus and not old ways. And that's where the healing and the glory and the fresh starts come. To this moment, I'll choose progress and blisters over safe and reliable any day. Today, it's okay to say goodbye to something old you've relied on. Thank those shoes for every step, and slip into the new things you've learned, then boldly walk forward onto the path God has for you.

You Are Right Where You Are Supposed to Be

I can recall many times in my life when I didn't fit in, didn't belong, or maybe just *felt* as though I didn't belong—in school, the workplace, or even among friends. I'm sure we've all felt like the odd man out, like *wow, what am I doing here? Please, no one ask me a question, because I feel like you'll find me out!* Worried that the wisps of insecurity are visible and not just in your mind's eye. Reminding yourself it's okay: *Breathe, you got this...*

But know this: You aren't awkward. You are unique!

My job sometimes takes me to amazing places, and I've been very fortunate to meet some wonderful people. A short while ago, I was working on a podcast that ended up taking me to Sundance. As in—yes!—*the* Sundance Film Festival, in Park City, Utah. I purchased faux fur–lined snow boots and a snow coat! I couldn't believe I was actually headed to the most exclusive film festival in the United States. What does one *do* at Sundance?

The company I was working for had arranged accommodations, and I was paired up with some of the executives in a beautiful home where I had my own room and bathroom. I already felt nervous. *Don't be weird, Danielle. Just go with the flow.* It's one thing to meet powerful higher-ups in a company you work for but another thing entirely to stay in a vacation home with them!

Our first night there, I had no hard plans, but the ladies I was with were getting ready to go to dinner, a dinner with a secret special guest of honor. "Who is the guest?" I asked excitedly.

"Martha Stewart," they replied.

Without hesitation, I asked if I could go. An intimate dinner honoring the legend herself! I'd *love* to attend! But they didn't think I could attend. It was ticketed. I told them I completely understood. I felt silly after asking. What was I thinking? Obviously, they weren't just going to let *me* attend.

But I'm an asker. You'll never fully experience the world if you never ask if you can go. Because sometimes it's the *one thing* that ends up mattering in your story. Just asking, just taking that leap of faith. I can honestly say that simply *asking*, even when I felt like I wasn't good enough or talented enough, often turned out to be the thing that launched me or carried me forward and gave me an opportunity to learn and grow. And even fail, I might add.

And this was one of those cases where I had to ask. Though

I was a bit nervous, I had to gather the courage to say, "Can I come along?"

Later in the evening, there was a knock on my bedroom door. One of the executives said, "We were able to arrange a seat for you! Get dressed, and freshen up. You're headed to dinner with us."

Needless to say, I was thrilled! *Here I go,* I thought. I had brought a few outfits, but nothing fit for this sort of affair! I had a black silk blazer that I knew was too tight, but fortunately I had brought it anyway. Well, tight coat, it's your lucky night! I put it on and thought, *If I keep my arms down, maybe no one will notice I can't lift them!* I silently pleaded with the coat: *Please don't split at the back shoulder seams.* Then with God: *Please, God, help to keep this coat from splitting!*

We arrived at the venue, and it was electric! It was late as well. Dinner at 8:00 p.m. I'm a mom of two little kiddos, so normally we eat around 5:00, then it's baths and bedtime, and we are exhausted by 8:00 p.m. But this night, I was up for it!

When Martha arrived, the noisy room fell quiet. *She's here!* I thought. She wore this big, delicious, feathery outfit. Her entourage held a tight formation around her as she made her way to her table.

Dinner began, and the courses were absolutely lovely! The most memorable for me was a ravioli made with eggy pasta and filled with delicious, creamy cheese and chicken meat floating in a rich broth. Think chicken noodle soup, only wildly whimsical and even more comforting.

I tried to make small talk, but I just felt a little out of my league. There were actors and filmmakers and executives sitting around the table, and here I was just wishing I had more ravioli and a little more give in the arms of my coat. I wasn't chatting about the latest films; I was secretly scoping out the servers to see if they had another serving of pasta on hand. My own insecurities aside, however, I was having a lovely time.

The dinner went on, and several speakers, one after another, stepped to a microphone to honor Martha. Eventually, she stood up to speak just a few feet from my table. As the dinner came to an end, I felt blessed and fortunate to have been there. I noticed Martha began to make her way around the room greeting people. I tried to get snapshots with my phone, but it wasn't working out. The images were blurry in the low light. As she came closer to our table, I thought, *Okay, perfect. She's just behind me. I'll grab a snap!* I was attempting to take a selfie with her in the background when the unthinkable happened.

We made eye contact in the back lens of my phone's camera—I was caught! I gasped. Now, not only was Martha Stewart looking at me, the women who had brought me seemed a little uneasy that I was trying to covertly take pictures of Martha Stewart.

In two seconds, though, Martha had moved past her entourage and was walking toward me at a clip so fast I could hardly put my phone down. What had I done? She reached me, and I was tomato red, heart pounding. She nestled her head into my shoulder and said in an oh-so-Martha-Stewart voice, "Did we get it?" She had a huge playful grin, and immediately I tried to explain away my actions. She just quieted me and instructed me to get my phone back out to snap the picture. Which I did! She giggled, squeezed my shoulders, and walked toward the door with her group. A woman trailing behind Martha's entourage knelt down and whispered, "You must be special. She doesn't often do that."

The truth is that we all must be special. If I hadn't gathered the courage to ask if I could attend and if I hadn't pulled my phone out, I'd never have this fun story to tell. I never would have had the entertaining and recipe queen herself kneel beside me and whisper into my ear to snap the picture again.

I want you to ask for the job. Shoot your shot. Ask to come along. Ask a new friend to coffee. Get up the courage to stick out, to show up, to be there in spite of your tight coat. Go anyway! There is more value in just *living* than impressing the "right" people.

I will never forget that night, for obvious reasons. But also for the not-so-obvious reasons. I asked to go in my ill-fitting clothes, and the ask gifted me an experience so rare and precious. It's time to get the yes moments you've been longing for. Believe in who God says you are. You are good enough. You are right where you are supposed to be. Ask for the opportunity, whatever it is you're seeking, even if it's a no in the end. One hundred noes will produce a yes in there somewhere. The yes is a wonderful experience just waiting to enrich your life. Just ask!

Just Passing Through, or Chasing Home

The timer went off, and I pulled the chicken tortilla roll-ups from the oven. Just fifteen minutes earlier, I had received a text message: "Hey, Danielle! ETA on the roll-ups?"

Oh my gosh! My mind went into full panic mode. I had promised the producer of a national television show that I would photograph and send along the snaps for the roll-ups we would be making during a taped segment, and I had forgotten all about it! That week had been incredibly busy for Mike and me. We were doing ten to twelve shoots a day, we were trying to find a new place to live, and of course there's the whole parenthood thing!

I flew to the fridge to pull together the items needed for the roll-ups. They were due hours ago! I was knee deep in waffle batter, dirty dishes, and plans for what came next in the schedule. I quickly texted back: "Fifteen minutes out!" I got the roll-ups in the oven and baking, finished up my round of waffles, and then, just as the timer dinged, a song began to play over the speakers in my living room, a song about seeing the evidence of God's goodness all over our lives.

Listening to that song, tears filled my eyes, and my mind flashed forward a few weeks to the day my family would have to drive away from the house where we were living, a place I loved, a place that had been my home for close to three years. Home means so many things to me. It means safety, that I can be myself, fully feeling all the things, and it's a place I can raise my babies and love my husband. But this house was, sadly, a place I did not own.

The emotion in my heart was heavy, and I felt like I was giving back the keys to my safe place. We still rent our homes thanks to the fallout from losing our restaurant so many years ago, always saving and praying for a home that is our own, a place where landlords won't blindside us through text message at 10:00 on a weeknight with the news that they plan to move back in within thirty days. It was time to go, and this home had become a special place for me.

A few weeks prior to receiving the bad news from our landlord, a bear showed up and began wreaking havoc at our house. He'd hang out in the backyard at night and eat from my garden and poop everywhere and drag garbage all over the place. We hid our garbage and did what we could within our limited power to get him to move on, but he seemed to like our neighborhood. Reflecting on this new intruder, I stood on my porch in the September sunshine and had a realization: *It is time to go.* But my emotions kicked in immediately. *Go? Where?* This house was my home, the home of my dreams! My children loved it, and Mike loved it. I loved it. Everything about this place was what we'd always hoped for.

I compartmentalized and moved away from that feeling quickly. I wasn't going *anywhere.* This was a pandemic year. Everything was out of whack, and this house was my safe place, my security. We were model tenants. We had cared for every bit of this house for close to three years as if it were our own investment. Things had happened in my heart in this home. I was digging my heels in. My career and faith had grown in this home. My marriage worked through many obstacles here, and we had become even better together in this home. But then the text from the landlord came, and I finally had to listen to the message God was sending me with that pesky bear.

I asked God for his best. I was in the shower the next day, tears mixing with the water running down my face, and I said, "God, close every door we aren't meant to have open. Please open doors no man can shut, and protect my marriage and family."

We looked high and low and couldn't find a place that felt settled, where I felt God was leading us. We went to look at rental after rental, applying for all of them to no avail. The clock was ticking. We needed to find a place to live during our little photography business's busiest time of year.

When the clock had run all the way down, we looked at a house that offered a bit of possibility, but it was run-down, worn-out, and in desperate need of fresh paint, new carpets, and myriad repairs. To bring it up to snuff would require blood, sweat, tears, and plenty of money. I stood on the porch, dejected and trying not to cry. *Well,* I thought, *this is going to be it. We will take this house and do our best to fix it up.*

I looked out into the yard, and an overwhelming sensation washed over me. *I will go wherever you go.* That was the Holy Spirit softly letting me know that it was not a home that healed me; it was God. I had been afraid of moving somewhere new, thinking that perhaps the progress would stop, the healing would stop, the blessings would stop. My time with God's help had run out. Things I never knew pained my heart were showing up, and I was extremely uncomfortable.

I knew the pain of losing a home. When our restaurant closed years before and our home was sold, I endured emotional pain that I couldn't quite describe. Being made to leave your home creates an insecurity that leaves a mark on your heart. It had left a mark on mine that I had been unaware of until nine years later, when we had to leave the home we had come to love. All that trauma came back.

Standing on the porch of this possible new rental, a flood of peace and light overtook me. It wasn't going to be easy, but the same God that cared for Israel cared for me. The same God who had so tenderly loved me toward healing and joy was going to go anywhere I went. He was in this with me, and nothing was going to change that, least of all my *address*. I realized I had been chasing "home" as a means of safety and worth. If I could provide a place that was beautiful and comfortable, I was doing something right. But all the while, the Lord needed me to pursue Him instead and trust that He would provide.

And I couldn't merely *say* it. I had to live it.

The Lion Beside Me

Four months after my son Milo was born, some girlfriends and I attended a women's conference featuring a prominent Christian speaker and blogger. I felt winded just walking from the parking lot into the venue. My body had just been through the most intense trial. My water broke at thirty weeks, and Milo came eight weeks early. He spent his first five weeks of life in the NICU, and I spent a week in the ICU myself battling sepsis after his birth.

I'd never heard the keynote speaker present before, but I *love* a good pep talk, and I sure needed one in that moment. She spoke for an hour or so, and though it was enjoyable, there was something missing. I observed the other attendees. It seemed a broken crowd, a crowd of women who needed hope and peace. They needed to know that their Heavenly Father was right there with them in the trials. He was holding them in the trenches. He was waiting to quell their fears and fill them up. But hope, sadly, wasn't given this particular evening.

I kept wanting this talented speaker to use her platform to point these precious women—God's girls—back to Him. At the end of the evening, she painted a vivid verbal picture of a tribe of elephants. Up on the mega screen, a photo of an elephant tribe appeared for dramatic effect. She spoke about how when one of the female elephants is sick or giving birth, the other females will surround her for protection, so that nothing gets in the way of her healing or bringing a baby into the world. These elephants, she informed us, kick up dust. This cloud of protection can be seen for miles, and the one sweet girl in the center is thereby surrounded, untouchable, and safe. She can mend until it's her turn to be the protector for someone else in the tribe.

This picture caused the crowd to go wild. They began to clap and holler as she went on to explain that each woman in that room needed to find *their* tribe and provide protection for one another. Women in the audience held each other, nodding. The speaker asked the few thousand ladies present to stand with their tribe, to hold one another up. The crowd bought it hook, line, and sinker and were crying out.

In the commotion, I noticed one woman from my group take her leave. As she slipped away, I felt like I was the only one not caught up in the frenzy. I seemed to be the only one saying to myself, *C'mon, girl, now point 'em to Jesus. Let these girls know it's gotta go back to Him.* I sat and watched the tears, the hugs, the tribes holding up their girls, just as the speaker directed. But she never brought the message back around to the one who really matters.

Following the event, as we wandered out en masse, I couldn't stop thinking about everything I'd witnessed. We came upon a woman weeping in the hallway; it was the woman from our group who'd slipped away as the conference was coming to a close. As we approached, she cried, "I don't have a tribe. I never had a tribe. While I battled cancer this last year, no one rallied around me. I had no support. Where were my elephants? Why didn't God bring my elephants?"

I didn't know her very well, and she wasn't speaking directly to me, so I didn't feel it was my place in that moment to speak up. But something was happening within my heart. This was my first night out since Milo's birth. He was just fourteen weeks old, and my body still hurt all over. The sepsis had left me healing slowly, with little stamina. The nearly yearlong bed rest prior to his birth had left me weakened. None of these ladies fully knew the details regarding the trauma and pain I'd experienced surrounding Milo's pregnancy, delivery, and birth. Milo and I had barely survived.

I listened to the crying woman's grievances with God. I couldn't help but relate to her. I too felt alone while sick with my pregnancy. Where were my close friends? Where had my people gone? One friend told me I was the strong one, so I likely didn't need help. But my husband worked fifty-five hours a week outside the home, then came home to keep up on the housework. I felt useless and lonely. The TV was babysitting my sweet five-year-old. I still had to earn a paycheck and often worked from my bed on a laptop computer.

During this time, I relied on God in a new way. I'd cry myself to sleep some days, wishing someone would help me clean my bathroom or care for my son. I was instructed by my doctor not to lift a finger. The pregnancy was delicate. No bending, no cleaning, no cooking. But I still had to live with no help. That year, my lonely year, God taught me to rely on Him alone. He taught me that sometimes He loves us so much that He draws us away to a lonely place where only He can impact or touch our lives. He draws us away to be alone solely for His glory to be revealed in our lives. He allowed that barren season, four seasons of winter, to heal my heart in ways I never could have dreamed. Four seasons of winter to bring our Milo into the world. I had to do this work quietly, alone.

It was during this time that I became resolved to finish my second book. I had self-published my first cookbook, and I had ideas and recipes in mind for my second, but there was no hard plan in place for its completion. The night before I was discharged from the ICU, I felt it was time to write again. I questioned God: *Huh? I am sorta clinging to the ledge right now. How am I going to write a book?* I told Mike my plan, and he was equally puzzled but never deterred me. He just said, "Okay, let's do it!"

The quiet time I'd experienced and the deep pain I had gone

through during the birth of my second son paved the way for me to begin writing, usually at night while my family slept. I was not distracted; I was filled with purpose. By mid-November, just four months after Milo was born, it was done. That book helped to heal me. God used that lonely year to prepare my soul and give me the strength to pour out a very special book: a cookbook about home, memory, and growing up.

Please don't misunderstand. We need our friendships, and we need to feel loved and supported. There have been seasons in my life brimming with healthy, loving relationships, with people who come alongside me to help and surround and love. But sometimes, in our darkest nights and loneliest mornings, the one we have to rely on is Him.

That night, after the conference, as I drove home, I prayed and thought. And it was as if flashbulbs began to go off. We simply don't need a tribe of elephants surrounding us in certain seasons; there will forever be a lion stationed beside us. The King of the World, the Prince of Peace. The Lion of Judah with my name written on His palm is stationed beside me through every trial. A lion commands far more respect than a gaggle of elephants. A lion doesn't need a dust cloud to ward off predators. The lion needs no pomp and circumstance to protect me.

I got home and immediately called the friend who had invited the crying woman to the conference with us. I asked, "Would you please call her? Can you paint this picture? Tell her, who needs the heifers when you've got the king of beasts beside you? You were never alone. God saw fit to be your sole source of strength because He loves you that much." A lion was beside her in every trial.

We all go through seasons. Seasons of joy, of sorrow, seasons flush with friends pouring into our lives, and seasons that see us crumpled each night, crying out of the brokenness and the desire to be cared for. Sometimes we yearn so deeply for something to satisfy our ache, something that might not even be found in this world. Our Heavenly Father loves us so much that in those crumpling times, He will never leave or forsake us. He will be there, positioned to protect. He will be our ever-constant provider in times of need. If you are feeling alone, if this time in your life has left you broken and needing hope, I am praying at this very moment that you will feel the peace of Jesus wash over your soul. That you will know there is a lion beside you. You can keep every elephant and their dust cloud from here to eternity. Just allow the Lion of Judah, Jesus, to be your herd of elephants.

Opinions, Opinions Everywhere!

When I was very young, maybe thirteen years old, I attended a youth conference at the Yakima Sun Dome convention center. I remember I could barely see the stage, but I felt so grown-up. I was so excited to hear about Jesus.

During this time in my life, I never quite fit in at school. I was endlessly in trouble for proclaiming all the injustices I saw on a daily basis. I got in fights with other kids. I was always defending the underdog. I'd get in anyone's face to declare my truths. I demanded people hear me! I was born with opinions about life and the world, and I lacked all finesse.

At the conference, a pastor approached me and said that I would speak to the masses one day, that I would minister to women's hearts. I never forgot that man or that prophecy. I had no idea how, over the next twenty years, I would be trained, shaped, and refined. When God makes a promise, He always keeps it.

A short time ago, I had a dream that I was in a crowded lunchroom standing on a table, and there were hundreds of people around. I was yelling out to this crowd, struggling to be heard, and no one would even acknowledge me. I was exhausted and exasperated, and I just kept on, losing my voice and shouting my message without so much as a head turn from anybody. They all just shuffled about, unaware I was there. When I had reached peak frustration, a gentleman walked up to me. He was shirtless for some reason! Aren't dreams great? He seemed pretty comfortable, so I just went with it. He put his hand on my shoulder and said, "When it's time, they will listen." As he walked away, I sat down, dejected, feeling a little lost. Then I woke up.

When it's time, they will listen. What a profound lesson. Timing is absolutely everything, and I've learned over the years that I don't want it if God's timing isn't right. Sometimes we strain and shout and try so hard, spinning our wheels to get anyone to listen. The truth is, maybe it's not time. When it's time, it'll happen. This notion correlates to so many areas in my life. I couldn't possibly plant a tulip bulb in December and expect a bloom in January. In fact, that tender bulb with a bloom inside has to overwinter. It has to be covered with soil, and the earth must fall dormant. The very ground that protects it will freeze, and it'll be six months before the green tulip leaves will break the surface. It won't bloom until the time is right. There is beauty in the waiting, in the softening. It's humbling to think back on my life and about what a turd I've been at times with my words. As it turns out, I wasn't called to spout my opinions off, though it feels good at times. I am called to speak about hope and joy and God's goodness in every situation.

One day as we drove our son Noah to school, he complained about writing and reading and all the tasks he must complete in class. I explained to him that those subjects were a gift and that I too complained away much of my schooling. But, I told him, somehow words had become my calling. I could never write, much less convey beautifully strung together thoughts or sentiments full of hope and encouragement, while in school. But God's timing is everything, and He saw fit to help me and guide me and train me to use words for His glory. I've heard it said that our greatest strength is also our greatest weakness. We must go through proper training in order to use our gifts.

I've always lived my life intensely loving people. I used to live my life intensely sharing my opinions with people, whether solicited or not. My big mouth has cost me many a friendship, because for so many years, I had, naturally, *always been right*! Unfortunately, even if I had been right, the message was undermined by my poor delivery.

I was at the beach with dear friends recently, and as we sat across from one another, we chatted about life and the past and told funny stories. I mentioned that I thought I was a lot more tender in how I shared my opinion than I had been fifteen years ago—heck, even ten years ago. I had graduated from the need to hear my own voice and tell everyone how misguided they were, even if I firmly believed it. My husband chimed in and said, "Oh yeah, you are *much* less inclined to spew your thoughts all over the place." That, he continued, was what had cost me *this* relationship and *that* friendship.

At first, his comment stung, but then I realized it was quite a compliment. I had allowed a softening of my heart. He was right. I had gone through some hard things, and in those fires, I'd learned how to have more grace for people. We are all working through something. Thankfully, God was merciful and loved me enough to show me what speaking truth in love really meant. It's not meant to be my truth. It's meant to be God's truth in love, and He is fully capable of changing hearts without my judgmental spin. This doesn't mean I'm not supposed to speak up, of course. Although God blessed me with the gift of communication, I had to learn how to properly use that gift. It's taken years of training, and I still inevitably fail now and again. Now, I understand that what I'm meant to share is less about what I feel is right or wrong and more about hope and love and peace in the Lord. I know that to minister to anyone's heart with the words of Jesus, I have to first humble myself before the Lord and acknowledge that apart from Him, I'm not very much. That in Him, I have hope and joy and the ability to see the forest through the trees. That no matter what happens in life, be it painful and extremely difficult, we can always find our strength and peace and joy in Jesus.

So you'll find me these days making people laugh and loving them, urging them toward hope. And let me tell you, funny hope is a much nicer place to work from than impassioned personal certitude. It's a place where I more easily recall the truth: when it's time, they will listen. And as with everything else in life, timing is everything.

Tuesdays with Gloria

It was the busiest of weeks. I was preparing to make fudge for the teachers' cookie exchange at Noah's school. I'd been assigned crinkle cookies, but my week had swiftly gotten away from me, so I emailed the exchange coordinator and said, "Hey, I need to change my entry to fudge!"

She dismissively said, "Oh, sorry, we've already got fudge!"

I wrote her back quickly and said, "Well, you've got two choices. We can have doubles, or I can participate next year and bow out this time." I didn't get the warmest response.

"Fudge will be fine," she replied.

Ugh, I made a PTA mother irritated. Ugh, I need to maintain this relationship!

"Okay," I wrote back. "I'll do the ding-dang crinkles. Nobody wants that much fudge."

She replied, "No, really, fudge is fine."

Whew! I didn't want to make crinkles. The morning the sweets were needed, I set out to make a magic three-ingredient fudge I'd seen floating around the internet. It consisted of sweetened condensed milk, chocolate, and nuts! That's it! My regular fudge recipes are awesome, but I always love to try new hacks.

Well, it bombed. I tried again, adjusting my temps and adding the condensed milk first this time. Again, a mess. The chocolate seized. I tried a third time. Surely, this must be a mistake? Catastrophe. There I was, exhausted and pressed for time and now out of chocolate. I just stood there and cried. I called my mother, who was at work. She said, "Honey, put peanut butter in them."

I said, "No, Mom, it's not like that. It's an oily mess."

She prayed for me and said, "Lord, help Danielle figure out how to save this."

I returned to the kitchen, still upset. After a moment, I left the kitchen once again and sat down to call my gramma Gloria. I left a long and rambling message about fudge and how I missed her and how I just needed to hear her voice.

I was grateful I still had a grandmother to call. She's well into her eighties, and she makes glorious fudge. Every Tuesday, she runs a local food pantry at her church. She's a lovely lady, and I was so weepy and grateful in that moment that she was still here with me. She's focused and driven and tells how she wakes up and thanks the good Lord for just one more day. She's seen some living in her days, and she's here for me to call during fudge disasters.

I went back into the kitchen and transferred two broken batches of fake, easy fudge into my stand mixer. I turned it on and began adding eggs. Slowly, the crumbly, oily, chocolate mess began to turn smooth. All of a sudden, it looked like a molten cake batter! I added sugar, vanilla, salt, and butter. I folded in flour and stuck the entire thing in the fridge to rest. I had inadvertently ended up making a crinkle cookie recipe in the longest, worst, most emotional way possible.

I started rolling the dough into balls, and Gramma Gloria called back. She loves to hear my stories. We talked about fudge, the food bank, and my babies. We talked about Milo's wild hair and Gramma Gloria's sister Charlotte. We talked about how I have a good man and how she never had that. How Mommy and Sissy and I picked wonderful husbands and how she's never known that sort of love. Then she laughed in her raspy and sweet way and said, "Okay then, go make your family dinner! I'll talk to you soon."

I hung up the phone and cried yet again. These moments that steal our joy and derail our thoughts can have the sweetest endings, if we allow them. If we just leave the kitchen and call members of our family. I realize how much time with my grandmother is precious. I know I want to know all about her life, and I want to remember to call her and tell her I love her fudge and zucchini bread. I want to tell her I admire her hardworking life and all she embodies.

The cookies turned out fine. Nothing earth-shattering, but just fine. Later, I worked on the recipe to create something really special (you'll find *that* recipe below). I happened to have a giant jar of Nutella in the house, as one does, obviously. I stuffed the well of each cookie with a teaspoon of happiness. A touch of salt sealed the deal!

I looked at my table with dozens of cookies strewn about it, and I was grateful. Grateful for happy accidents in the kitchen. Grateful for tears and for time with my grandmother. Now, when you set out to make these, just remember to give someone a call and listen to them speak. We learn in the listening.

Nutella Crinkle Thumbprints

PREP TIME: *15 minutes* • INACTIVE TIME: *30 minutes* • BAKE TIME: *10–12 minutes* •

YIELD: *Roughly two dozen*

2 cups bittersweet chocolate chips,
   melted and cooled but still pourable

1½ cups sugar

½ cup butter, softened

4 eggs

1 teaspoon vanilla extract

½ teaspoon kosher salt

1 cup all-purpose flour

¼ cup unsweetened cocoa powder

2 cups confectioners' sugar,
   for rolling the cookies

1½ cups Nutella

Flaky sea salt, for sprinkling over top
   (optional)

Place the melted chocolate in the bottom of your stand mixer, add the sugar and softened butter, and mix slowly. Add the eggs, and mix until everything just comes together. Add the vanilla and salt, then add the flour and cocoa powder. Combine, then chill the dough for 30 minutes.

Preheat the oven to 350°F. Using a half-ounce cookie scoop or a spoon, scoop the dough, and roll into balls. Roll the dough balls in the confectioners' sugar, and place on a cookie sheet. Press your thumb into each cookie to form a well. Bake cookies for 10 to 12 minutes. Allow to cool completely, then fill each cookie with 1 teaspoon of Nutella, and sprinkle with flaky sea salt (if desired).

A Journey in Chicken Salad

The last ten years have been a journey. We started out in a place, moved far away, and then moved again to end up right back where we started. I didn't think it was supposed to be like this. I used to think you never go back to where you started from. That would be going backward. Home reminds me of rest and healing. The city where I live now represents a time in my past that became really hard, and back then. I feel almost as if I came back to make things right in my heart.

When we moved for the third time in eight years, I did a familiar thing. I packed my kitchen up and sat in an empty house. It was to be paper plates and takeout for the last few days of the move. Mike picked up chicken salad from our local grocery store deli.

When I was pregnant with Noah years ago, I'd have Mike stop at the deli and get me a chicken salad sandwich and banana cream pie. It was such a splurge, and we were careful where every penny went, but when you are pregnant, you need *some* foods like you need air or water! He'd bring home a delicious sandwich with red leaf lettuce, whole grain bread, dilly chicken salad, red onions, and sometimes tomatoes. Something about that chicken salad was such a treat. I had no idea what was in store for us. We were going to have a baby, and our restaurant was closing its doors at the time. We were kids, clueless and unprepared. But when I look back, I have this deep nostalgia. It wasn't all bad and awful. We were just making our way through life. And I can remember special, wonderful moments, times when no matter what the uncertainty, joy had a place in our hearts and home. Like when we'd eat chicken salad sandwiches and banana cream pie together, expecting our baby, trying to make the failing restaurant work, just trying to figure life out, and anticipating our future together.

We had Noah, and that next year, we moved to Issaquah, Washington, to start fresh, baby in tow and wide-eyed, expecting good things. Noah brought us such joy. Now a family of three, we'd swing into the deli often and grab those same sandwiches.

Nostalgia plays a huge part in my life. Memories for me are reminders that life is, was, and will continue to be good. Even during painful times, life is good. I've based my entire life's work on believing in God's promises.

After five years in our little apartment in Issaquah, we were ready to move on and into a house. After all, there were four of us now, little Milo, the sweetest baby, joining our ranks. There we were, packing up our home again, embarking on that next phase, a fresh chapter. And Mike, always on board for engaging in nostalgia, would swing into the deli and grab a pound of dill chicken salad, sustenance for moving out.

Our lives had been reimagined at this point; we were long miles away from where we originally thought we'd be. We were raising two boys now, and we'd had many adventures while living in that little apartment. I walked those halls for the last time and turned in our keys. I can't help but think that that apartment is where our family *truly* began. There, more than anywhere, is where we learned to love each other in the best way. Inside those walls, we'd grown together and fought hard to keep it going. For us, chicken salad, by this point, had become emblematic of that growth.

Food will always evoke strong memories and emotion for me. I bet you never thought anyone could cry about chicken salad, but these dang sandwiches remind me of hope and God's plan. If any food has the ability to remind me to hope, man, then I'll take it.

We had many more ups, downs, adventures, and moving life experiences in our new home before it was time to go after nearly three years there. During the summer just prior to our last move, I attended my soon-to-be sister-in-law's bachelorette party. Someone in her family made these delightful chicken salad sandwiches to pack along on a beach day. Unwrapping my sandwich, so many memories came flooding back! I considered how she was being welcomed into our family and what a gift that was. Chicken salad seems to say goodbye and hello to new adventures for me. Also, I might add, that particular version of chicken salad is much tastier than mine, and I've since started making it their way.

Starting over isn't easy. We fail, we cry, and we are embarrassed sometimes, but we have to keep going. We go through loss of homes, jobs, and marriages, and sometimes those we love the most move on and into heaven, leaving a void so empty we feel as if nothing could quite fix our hearts. And during all of it, we eat. We eat to move on, we eat to get full, we eat to forget, we eat to heal, and we eat to remember. We have a bowl of soup or a slice of cake or a burger or fries like our mama made. We eat chicken salad sandwiches to remember moving on from our kitchens and that we don't know what tomorrow brings, only that we are going there with the Lord's help.

The week I wrote this, I made chicken salad. I, Mike, and the boys have moved back to my hometown. It's a healing time. I feel it. I toasted some bread and piled it high. Loads of dill and dried cranberries and green onions and a bit of Greek yogurt, all alongside mayo for extra creamy goodness. I thought about how we are home again, eating a fresh version of the chicken salad I'd enjoyed through so many transitional years. I'm a fresh version of myself. Time has added so many layers and uncovered so much good stuff.

The chicken salad is like that. I've continued to perfect the recipe I've loved for so many years, adding new ingredients, switching ingredients out, and fine-tuning with every incarnation.

Life isn't about arriving at the destination; it's about all the things we do on the way there and sharing our stories, for each one is a lesson to pass on. It's about adding layers and new flavors as we go, all the while keeping on keeping on.

For me, life keeps coming back to food. Food experiences have shaped me, and I've tried to recount those experiences to help shape others, leading them toward hope. Eating my chicken salad sandwich this week, I sat near the window, at peace. I don't know what the future holds, but I intend to be present and fully *in* each moment.

I hope you make chicken salad and say hello to a big wide-open future. Put your trust and hope and desire in Jesus. He's a good friend, a protection, and an ever-present help along the way.

Chicken Salad

PREP TIME: *30 minutes* • BAKE TIME: *25–30 minutes* • YIELD: *Roughly 8 cups*

4 boneless skinless chicken breasts (roughly 2 pounds)

1 tablespoon olive oil

1 tablespoon all-purpose salt-free seasoning blend

Salt and pepper to taste

1½ cups Greek yogurt

1 cup mayonnaise

1 cup dried cranberries, chopped

1 cup sliced almonds

½ cup chopped fresh dill

½ cup finely diced flat leaf parsley

3 to 4 green onions, sliced

2 to 3 ribs celery, diced

1 teaspoon onion powder

Salt and pepper to taste

Preheat the oven to 350°F. Lay the chicken breasts on a baking sheet lined with parchment paper, drizzle with olive oil, and season with salt-free seasoning and salt and pepper. Bake for 25 to 30 minutes or until the chicken reaches 165°F internally. Allow to cool enough to dice.

Add the remaining ingredients to a mixing bowl, and place in the fridge while chicken cooks and cools. Dice the chicken, and add to the mixing bowl. Mix and taste for seasoning. Store in the fridge. Salad keeps up to 4 days. Add a few extra tablespoons of mayo if you'd like more dressing in the mixture the next day.

A Restful Shift

Just a couple of years ago, I filled all my free time with my business, book events, and peddling my wares. I tried hard to provide for our family, and I didn't quite know what burnout really felt like. We were in survival mode and pouring every bit of everything we had into Rustic Joyful Food.

Every effort paid off, so it led to more effort. I worked my regular job and had a trade-off schedule with Mike. I'd normally get home after the boys ate dinner, around 6:00 or 7:00, and we'd jump into bedtime routines. I can remember when Noah was small and we started eating dinner at the table together as a family. Now that he was a big boy, it was important for me to be home from work to eat dinner with him. My schedule didn't always allow for that, so sometimes Mike and Noah would drive into downtown Seattle to pick me up so we could spend more time together.

During that time, my priorities began to shift. I'd need to adjust so I could be home for dinnertime. As I transitioned from working outside the home to running our business full-time, it was better for my family, but I never set work-life balance boundaries. Even now, I sustain a seven-day workweek, even if only a couple of hours a day. When the pandemic hit, it helped me set boundaries. During those first few turbulent months, when we had several jobs canceled and I was fearful of a significant loss of income, we slowed down as a family.

I didn't anticipate that. I had no idea what "slow down" really meant. It felt foreign. It felt wrong to be still for a few hours. It led to these strange, unhappy feelings. As time went on and life began to settle back into a more familiar routine, with Noah back in school and clients pivoting back to us, I realized something important: I'll never work that hard again. I'll never sacrifice my body for my calling or my sleep for a few extra dollars. Sometimes God repeatedly reminds us what's important for years until we finally get it.

A few years ago, I sat in the lobby of the Opryland Hotel in Nashville waiting for a car to arrive and whisk me off to a television appearance. I was weary. I felt achy, and my body was tired. I watched a few children playing across from me and missed Noah. In that moment, I told the Lord I was tired of striving, of working so hard. I closed my eyes and felt the Holy Spirit whisper to my soul: *You don't have to try so hard. I have not forgotten you.* I tilted my head upward to save the tears from taking my makeup with them as they fell into my lap.

Relief washed over me.

I called my mom and told her how I felt this new burst of peace and energy, nothing wild, but a settled feeling. I didn't have to try so hard. I can see the hand of my savior in my life at every turn, in every decision. Why was I spinning my wheels when He was so kind and at the helm every step of the way?

I went into that TV appearance with a fresh perspective. I met people that weekend who changed my life. I know now that if I hadn't surrendered to the Holy Spirit and settled that truth deep into my heart, I wouldn't be where I am right now. When I think of that day, I am reminded to come back to a place of peace.

Act on the soft and gentle leading of your heart. I believe these gentle nudges are the work of the Holy Spirit. Get up and go for a walk. Speak kindly to yourself. Bless a friend with groceries. I know that God speaks gently to our hearts and minds, and the more we act on His leading in obedience, we are better able to decipher His callings in our lives. We are more equipped to receive His goodness. I never want to miss the goodness of the Lord by being too hurried or up in my head, too busy to make it through the day in peace, missing all He has to offer. Sometimes it's just as simple as drinking in the sunshine and giving thanks for His mercies.

I remembered that time in the lobby of the hotel, and that feeling came back to me. I remembered when I needed to shift my work schedule when Noah was small. During the pandemic, I decided that my family needed more of me. It was time to shift again. These waves of exhausted sadness had only one solution: I needed to rest—not in bed but in my mind. My journey has taught me that rest in your mind is far more valuable than rest in any bed. To be able to turn down the worry and fear and endless questions is far more restorative than any great night's sleep. But I do love sleep.

When my mother was in the thick of raising her four children, often overwhelmed by life, she'd feel these waves of sadness come over her. She told me they'd come while doing dishes. Thoughts and feelings would creep in, and by the time she was done, she'd be worked into this sad, upset state. This went on for some time. She told me how one day, as those feelings came over her, she said, "No more." She would no longer side with the enemy about her life. She would no longer allow these thoughts to oppress her. She told me, "Danielle, it's not that those feelings stopped coming. It's that I stopped holding court for them. I stopped giving them life."

This last year during the pandemic, it took a lot for me to stop giving negative feelings precedence in my mind. Just a few months ago, we stopped working on the weekends. Perhaps that sounds unrelated to negative feelings, but giving myself and my husband two days in a row away from the grind was something we hadn't done in ten years, and it has significantly lessened the impact of those negative feelings. I'm not saying it's a hard-and-fast rule, but generally we treat weekends as rest and family time. That's big for this workaholic! I draw value from working, and it had become time to draw value from resting as well. Just like so many years before, when I needed to shift my makeup schedule to accommodate dinnertime with Noah, it was time to shift again to address my family's needs, and we desperately needed boundaries.

I didn't make any announcements. I just stopping setting up our work days on the weekend. Mike is the greatest and hardest worker. He is ready and willing to do anything he's been asked, so my nature is to ask. We never stop. I hadn't seen how hard that was on our relationship until I pulled back. At first, the time felt like fresh air, but then I noticed that peace and joy were more abundant. No guilt for not logging on to the computer. We've always been a family that goes on drives or out to dinner, and we spend a great deal of time with family and friends. But I had learned to pack work in around downtime, every day of the week from morning to night. I approached my job with this must-get-it-all-in-today mentality.

Looking back, I don't feel any guilt, but I do feel keenly aware that I am able to get just as much done while making space for real rest. I'd say our productivity is much higher, more well-rounded. And setting boundaries for myself, my marriage, and my work has produced a happier home life.

If things feel off in your heart, let me urge you to take stock of how you are spending your days. I wasn't even truly aware my days had become devoted primarily to work. Some things we cannot change in a moment, such as our jobs or where we live. But we can make small choices that lead to big, healthy change. There are these immediate things we can do. We can choose to no longer hold court for the feelings that cripple us or freeze progress. You will get to where you are going at the perfect rate. If you say no along the way at the right moments, you might just get there more peacefully. Open your heart to addressing all the components of your life that require attention. You might also find yourself getting a lot more done within your boundaries. Make enough time for your children, your spouse, your parents or grandparents. They need you now more than ever.

The work can wait its turn.

Glowing Motherhood

I found a picture of myself the other day. In it, I stood before a wall covered in bougainvillea in San Diego. The flowers are a deep magenta, and they scale walls and trees and sidewalks all over Southern California. They're like a welcoming committee, the way they cheerfully greet you at every turn. I have always been in love with the bougainvillea.

The photo was taken nearly three full years ago, from the time of this writing. Milo was all of eight months old and about the size of a four-month-old. Noah was six and darling. I felt so unattractive. It was a time in my life when I wasn't appreciating what my body had done, what it had gone through to get my kids here. I remember packing for that trip feeling completely overwhelmed by my appearance and feeling ugly. Mike reassured me constantly, "You look great, babe." I didn't feel great. "Please don't say terrible things about yourself," he'd say. I couldn't help it. All I saw in the mirror was this overweight, unattractive, tired lady. This old lady.

I think motherhood sometimes leaves us feeling this way. All this lack of sleep, stress, and trying to do it all. I had a full-time job running our business and a full-time job raising these kiddos. I was learning how to heal this sad part of myself I'd just met following Milo's birth. Michael had just left his secure job of fifteen years to work on our business. It was the Wild West for us, scary and wonderful at the same time.

As I held this photo of myself, I replayed the trip in my mind. It was wild for sure. We had flown to California for a TV appearance. After the appearance, we headed to Disneyland! Always on a tight budget, I packed snacks for the trip. I'd booked us into an economy hotel right across the street from Disney for the night. It was a super dive, by all means, but the price was right. It was close to the park and clean (I hoped).

At the time, Noah was notorious for getting sick if he ate the slightest bit too much junk food, and traveling had us eating more fast food and convenience snacks than normal, to say the least. Sure enough, this kid christened the bathroom royally the first night in that hotel. In spite of this and the fact that the place was sort of a dive, we loved it! It was an adventure after all.

The next morning, after a night of handling the mess of Noah's sensitive tummy and spotty sleep otherwise, I noticed the kids and

I were covered *all over* in itchy, red dots. A quick search revealed a tiny, jumping, black bug on Noah's leg: a flea!

I put on socks and shuffled the carpet, a little trick I learned growing up with loads of pets. I examined the socks, and, sure enough, our hotel room was infested. We called the front desk, mortified. They said it's not that uncommon, and I was like *get me outta here!*

Half laughing and half crying but relieved it wasn't bedbugs, we figured we'd head to San Diego, just pack up, get on the road, and pick up some Benadryl on the way. Mike's always up for an adventure, and the kids didn't mind one bit. We googled the best fish tacos in San Diego and found a really great deal on a beautiful hotel. We swung into this great taco place and ordered so much food. Saving on a day at Disneyland meant a bigger food budget, and Mike and I were in heaven! I held Milo and fed him a bottle while Mike fed me tacos. Noah loves Mexican food and enjoyed a burrito. Dream day! It was a special moment for our family, peaceful, sunny, and breezy. The ocean was the brightest blue.

But in spite of the lovely time we were experiencing, all the while, I just couldn't shake this feeling of inadequacy. It was a dark cloud hanging over everything.

Looking at this photo of myself, I began to really consider that San Diego trip in a way I hadn't up to this point. At one point in our exploring, we pulled off to the side of the road and Mike said, "Let me take a picture of you."

I protested. "No, I don't feel good. I don't look nice. I ate way too much."

He insisted and won. He said, "Okay, now look to the left and smile. I think you'll love it!"

I didn't love it. I thought *Wow, I've really changed.*

Holding this photo now, years later, those times feel like nothing short of bliss. I laughed to myself, remembering. I started looking at other photos: the tacos, the flowers, the babies, so tiny and scrumptious! Our children were little angels, and we made them— how hilarious! What a fun trip! We swam in the pool and ate more tacos and drove around the city in search of ice cream.

The following morning, we had to make a three-hour trip back to the airport. But first, we made one last sunrise trip to the beach and watched surfers riding, then crashing in the waves. Our hearts were full. These surfers were being repeatedly beaten by the surf, yet they continued to get up and paddle out again on their boards. It was inspiring. I remember telling Noah, "Just always get back up, buddy."

At the airport, we were settling to await our plane at the gate when we ran into some acquaintances who were heading home on the same flight. Their family of five had been vacationing somewhere exotic, like Brazil. This couple had taken three small kids to South America! We rolled into the airport that day like a hot mess. My kids' clothes never match, and I always seem to have messy hair and old tights on. When I saw this other family, it was like wind, light, and a singing choir conspired to guide their way down the concourse! The mother of this charmed family looked *stunning*, as if she had floated into the airport. Carrying a pack-and-play and carry-on luggage enough for five and wearing matching outfits, they looked so rested and put together. I was covered in spit-up, and my hair was greasy from our early wake-up; I was so embarrassed! I was likely wearing the shirt I slept in. Running into this seemingly enchanted family was just one more thing at the time to make me feel like poop. I thought, *How do I get that put together?*

They told us of their escapades in the jungle—again, *with small children in tow!* I told them we went to San Diego after our hotel room had fleas in it! Good one, Danielle. Great comparison. They were very kind and laughed along with us.

I couldn't help but laugh as I remembered this story! As our plane descended toward Seattle, my darling kids with sensitive stomachs began to throw up. Yes, both of them, in unison. They barfed on me. It was awful. When we landed, you could palpably sense the pity coming off the deboarding passengers as they passed. There was no hiding what had happened. Mike and I frantically got the kids cleaned up using thin, small, nearly worthless napkins and wipes, to no avail. We just had to get off the plane and to a restroom! As I stood up with Milo in my arms, covered in vomit, our friends were coming down the aisle.

Horrified, she said, "Oh gosh, are you okay?"

I said, "Well, both kids puked on me."

"Oh, wow. Do they have the flu?"

"No," I said, laughing to hold back tears. "Just a streak of good fortune!"

She didn't laugh and was genuinely concerned. I had to chuckle as we shuffled off the plane. The kids were ultimately fine, and nothing but my ego was really destroyed. We laughed on our way to the restroom, where I found a dirty but puke-free shirt to put on.

All these memories. What a hilarious, wildly fun vacation. One other thing stood out to me as I looked at that photo of me: It was beautiful. Wow! I was beautiful. I spent that trip feeling so down on myself, and I was so, so *beautiful*. My skin was glowing, my hair was windswept, and my million-dollar smile was bright. Young motherhood is glowing motherhood. It's raw and real and really gorgeous. It's full of insecurity, true, but you are literally conquering the world. All these emotions and memories flashed through my mind, swiftly and wonderfully.

I only thought about it all for a few minutes. And I made a promise to never let myself feel like that about my body or my motherhood again. That trip was glorious, and I'm sure we will laugh about it over dinner with our kids someday.

The things we think about ourselves can be extremely deceiving. That woman was merely concerned about us, and in the face of her compassion, I needlessly felt *not good enough*. The truth is, I was more than good enough. *You* are more than good enough. As I write this, I'm heavier than that day by a solid thirty pounds. My skin is filling with tiny wrinkles. My double chin is oh-so-double-double. But I know that we are living in the most magical time right now. And babies don't keep; children don't keep. They will never be as small as they are at this moment, so I will champion my body and my glowing motherhood. Because someday when my hair has silvered, my cheeks have lost their apples, my mouth is framed by deep lines, and my fingers are bent from life, I will hold the photos of the woman I am right now and think, *Gosh, she is beautiful. Gosh, this family and life that God gave me are beautiful.*

Love every moment, love every stage, and refuse the lies that would rob you of your peace, joy, and memories. Today, in my chubby body, I am so dang pretty. And so are you, mama! Life doesn't rob us of our bodies. Our images aren't ruined by changing. They're enriched and secured by living life to the fullest. Be kind to them. Cherish them. Feed them lots of veggies and water and slices of chocolate cake every so often, and revel in the miracle that is parenthood.

I realized that I am the queen of my boys' hearts until they find their wives. A queen should always carry herself in high esteem so that the tiny princes will always treasure their wives at every stage and size in their lives.

I printed that photo. I put it on my desk, and with every glance, I remember fish tacos and fleas and a damn good time with my kids and husband. I'll never again give life to the part of myself that thought negatively of my much younger, smoother body. Go easy on yourself, and if you need a reminder that you are beautiful and strong, show up in pictures of yourself. One day, the pictures you are in will become a soothing balm for the day you might be living through. You are beautiful at every stage. Simply glowing.

To make sure you're enjoying life to its absolute limits, here is the chocolate Bundt cake recipe you'll need, in addition to all that water and those fruits and veggies. Balance is beautiful.

Brown Butter Chocolate Bundt Cake

PREP TIME: *10 minutes* • BAKE TIME: *45–50 minutes* • MAKES: *1 9-inch Bundt pan*

1 cup butter

1 cup unsweetened cocoa powder

2 cups all-purpose flour

2 cups sugar

4 eggs

1 tablespoon baking powder

½ teaspoon kosher salt

2 tablespoons vanilla extract

½ cup Greek yogurt or sour cream

1 cup chocolate chips

Preheat the oven to 350°F. Brown the butter in a saucepan over medium heat; this takes roughly 5 minutes, until the butter is foamy and golden brown in color. Add the butter to the bowl of a stand mixer or mixing bowl. Add the cocoa powder, and mix. Add the flour, sugar, eggs, baking powder, salt, and vanilla, and mix. Add the yogurt or sour cream, and mix until the batter just comes together. Add the chocolate chips, and mix just a touch more to incorporate. Bring 1 cup of water to a boil in the same saucepan you used to brown the butter, then add to the batter, and mix for 20 to 30 seconds until completely mixed but not overmixed.

Pour the batter into a buttered or sprayed Bundt pan. Place in the oven, and bake for 45 to 50 minutes or until the cake is set in the center, or when tiny bits of cake come out on a toothpick.

A New Day Breaks at Midnight

There is an on-fire, trailblazing, do-it-scared, let's-go, don't-look-back, full-speed-ahead woman inside me who is desperate to tell you that *you are worth more than you ever imagined.* That every inch of your body is worthy. That every ounce of your flesh is called. That every hell you've had to walk through and every burden you've been weary while carrying has all been to let you know that *you were always here.*

You've never lost you.

You've never been so caught up in work or motherhood or loss that the trailblazing, fearless, incredibly unique woman you are has ever not been *exactly* where you're called to be at each and every moment in your life. This life you've been given is raw.

It's rough. It'll knock the wind out of you when you are minding your business. There will be cuts so deep that the tears you cry to relieve your ache will burn your cheeks. There will be nights that feel as though they may never end.

During the pandemic, our little company, Rustic Joyful Food, like so many companies, struggled mightily. Our jobs were drying up. Then a sweet friend bought a private cooking class from me for $2,500. We needed that money. At 12:02 a.m., she made her purchase and sent me a text that said, "God hasn't forgotten you."

I realized we were in the first minutes of a brand-new day. Even though it was the darkest part of the night, I was awake and soaking in the promise of a new day. I'd heard gospel singer Rita Springer say once that each new day breaks at midnight, during the darkest hour, but it's brand-new.

Never forget that in your darkest place, there is a new life about to begin. This is your glorious comeback. To live knowing who you are is your solid reminder that God doesn't make junk. He has called you for His glory. He has set you apart. He has offered to carry you while you rest leaning on His shoulders. You are gifted. You are beautiful. You are one of a kind. The sooner you start believing who God says you are, the sooner you will walk in freedom. Not in ease, but with the King of the Universe. Even as you are saddled with your burdens, He is acquainted with your grief. You, my darling girl, have never been lost. You were always there, waiting to step into the fullness of who you were created to be, free from noise and outside distractions. A badass conqueror!

You are precious. You are generous, and you are doing the best you can with what you've got. Open your arms, tilt your head to the heavens, drink in the sweet air, and stand in the fullness He has created you for. Let go of the what-ifs and remember-whens. This season is *go* season, your growing season. This is your I-am-worthy season. And if this is your lonely season, I promise you that you've never been alone, only set apart for glory. Walk in it. Revel in it, and put one foot in front of the other.

We are living in an age when there must be war in your intentions. Warring for good, for peace, for rest. And warring over the kingdom, you'll advance, by speaking the name of Jesus into the void and sharing the love and acceptance He offers. But you, darling girl, will ultimately realize that He's won this war already, just for you. Revel in the acceptance He has given and in real joy over who you are made to be. We weren't created perfectly and without flaws or failures, but in these inadequacies, we find our voices and need for Jesus and the people He has placed in our lives to shape us, grow us, and bring us hope.

Calling Out for Purpose

We have always been told that we have a calling in life. This is true. We all do. Maybe it's a call to motherhood or a call to service. Perhaps it's a call to be an employee at a company that makes canned green beans. I think we can have many callings. Our purposes can be found in our children's laughter, a hug, a clean kitchen, and freshly washed sheets. It can be found sharing what we have to eat with someone who needs food.

It might not seem important, but an honest day's work and caring for yourself is, in and of itself, a noble calling. I think that's what we all need to hear. This "one calling" idea has messed us all up a bit (me included). The myth that we have one true calling, that we've got to find the girl we once were to thrive is simply not sound. We are called to love Jesus, and through that calling, He uses us each day, gently and in different ways. Some days, it's through loving our babies or doing our laundry. Some days, it's through extending a kind word to a stranger. Some days, it's through doing our jobs well. I have found that the things that ignite my passions play a big part in my calling.

Sometimes we carry a heavy load, but that doesn't mean we aren't called to it. Looking back, I see now that during times of utter heartbreak and brokenness, my savior was not only present but using it for His glory in my life. Glory isn't always grand or stunning; glory can be subtle. It may be finally forgiving myself for something I said. Or an ugly feeling I'd had toward another person. Glory might be unpacking trauma and allowing Jesus to heal every broken, rejected place in my marriage or other important relationships. Glory may be the roads and trials we walk alone, without a comrade seemingly within miles. When we come up out of that wilderness, leaning on our lovers. When we are vulnerable enough to depend on Jesus for our every need.

That's the glory I believe I am living for. To be broken, poured out, and put back together with iron in my soul where there used to be flimsy beams. You are right where you are supposed to be at this moment. And if where you are feels hard and barren, I know it's not an easy pill to swallow. But I do know in my heart that joy shows up in mourning, and for every sorrowful season, we are entering into a beautiful, light-filled season of hope, ready to appreciate it with fervor and new eyes.

And all this merely *adds* another crucial layer to the woman you've always been. I don't believe you *can* lose who you once were. The woman you were has never been lost. She has just been collecting iron in the name of hope.

You Want Coffee Too? I Got You.

From the time Milo was born, we jumped straight back into work with little to no break. And after his time in NICU, adjusting to our new family of four was a legitimate struggle. But we were doing it! My sweet boy Noah worked desperately to find his new place in our family. I was tired all the time. The growing pains were hard. I felt some moments as if it was hard to breathe. The emotions of birth and life take a toll on a woman's heart.

I'd cry myself treasures. Yes, you read that correctly. I'd cry treasures: healing tears accompanied by lessons I'd come to find out can only be produced after a freeze, after what seems hopeless and barren and lifeless. Your treasure is coming. God remembers every trial. He turns them for His good! And treasures during this time were abundant. Being with my family was incredible. I wrote my second cookbook during this valuable time. Mike and I were working together and loving the process. And after we finished the book, we decided to send ourselves on a book tour.

I figured we'd start in New York, then head to California. I've always been our hype man. I was the publicist putting it all together. January arrived, and off we went, five-month-old baby in tow!

Here we were in NYC on a shoestring budget, feeling like it was exactly where God wanted us. In spite of that, there was no shortage of concern over where every penny needed to go. We had self-published, we had had a baby in the NICU, and we were putting our oldest boy through private school on financial aid. I packed everything we would need into one giant suitcase: clothes for three people. Noah stayed back home with my parents, and I packed enough to last a couple of days—toiletries, baby stuff, you name it. After landing at JFK, we shuffled outside and arranged for a car to whisk us off to our hotel in Manhattan.

When we arrived, it was dark, and we were on cloud nine! We were really doing it! I was fortunate enough to get a shot promoting our new book on a national television show.

"Babe," I said, "can you get Milo's clothes out of the suitcase? It's not in here." We had been upgraded to a two-room suite. What a treat! I checked the bedroom. No suitcase. It wasn't in the next room either. Mike quickly sprang into action. With only a hint of panic in my voice, I said, "The suitcase...where is it?" Must be in the lobby! Oh, gosh, we were forgetful these days, still recovering from the fog that was Milo's birth this past summer.

Mike came back from the lobby empty-handed. It wasn't there. I was pretty upset. We had left it somewhere! I yelled at Mike and called my mother. Mike made a two-hundred-dollar round trip Uber ride to JFK to look for our suitcase. I called every phone number I could find for the airport. Every department. No luck. Mike spent all evening there, filling out forms, chatting with the port authority officials, and asking anybody who might have seen the bag if they had, indeed, seen it.

No luck. He arrived back at the hotel, dejected. Meanwhile, I had told a few friends what happened, and they immediately sent me some money. Money? Yes! Money! My inner circle knew just how much was in that suitcase, and when you are in Manhattan, toiletries and undies alone for the week can set you back a hefty dollar amount! Everything I thought was important was in that bag. All my best clothes. I had meetings planned all week, and I had shopped for days to find the perfect outfit for my show appearance. And just like that, gone! So many people I told assured me it'd be found and returned.

I was devastated that night. I mourned the loss of my stuff and then, quickly, I let it go. It was just that: stuff. A bunch of stuff. Just a load of baggage that I needed to let go. Thinking about all my precious things as simply baggage made it really easy to say goodbye, to move forward with just the clothes on my back, and to buy only what I would need, nothing extra. I had overpacked for New

York. I had brought things I had no business bringing along, and the suitcase was heavy. I had trudged through the airport with all this stuff. So much baggage. How funny that the next day I couldn't help but consider everything I was dragging along in my life, all the bits and pieces of things I'd been through and hadn't let go of. All the hurt, all the heartache carefully folded between lovely memories and joy. All just dragged from one experience in my life to the next.

I asked the Lord to remove all the extra crap from my life in that hotel room. I gave him my baggage. I let it go. People were calling, concerned, after I made a quick social media post describing what had happened. But I closed the post with, "Luggage or not, there are goals to be crushed. And crush them we will."

The next morning, we brushed our teeth and hair and threw on the previous day's clothes. We put Milo in his stroller and headed out to find something for me to wear on TV. The sweet producer of the show made sure I had makeup, undergarments, and even toothbrushes.

We needed a good cup of coffee that morning to get our minds right. We stopped into a shop about a block from our hotel. Just ahead of us in line was a man who appeared to be homeless. The cold had been brutal in New York in the recent weeks, and this morning was no exception. He ordered a sandwich. The woman behind the counter told him his total, about seven dollars. He held out his cupped hand. In it, there was a dollar and some change.

He humbly said, "Ma'am, this is all I have, and I am hungry."

She didn't even hesitate. She boldly sang out, "I got you!"

He stood there quietly.

She leaned in and, this time, whispered it: "I got you." She held out a hand.

Her coworker quickly picked up on what was happening and said, "What are we drinking?"

"No, no, just the sandwich," he replied.

"Nah, nah, man, don't worry about it. What are you drinking? We got you today!"

He said he'd like a drip coffee.

The barista nodded and said, "Keep it movin', brother, I'll meet you at the end of the bar with your goods!"

The man shuffled forward, and we were next. I stepped out of line with the stroller to hide my tears. I was sobbing by this point. All I could feel was the gentle pressing of the Holy Spirit letting me know *I got you. Jesus has you. He's got you in the palms of His hands.*

You may very well be in the fight of your life, taking back your ground, rediscovering the you who's always been there, or being trained for who He called you to be. But there comes a point in time when you've got to put your money on the counter and say, "I'm hungry." You may feel like you don't have enough. But what you have is good. It's enough. God will meet your efforts and make up for every shortcoming. He will stand in the lack and make up for every area where you come up short. He won't just meet your needs; He will exceed all your expectations. You want coffee too? He's got you. He's got all you need. He's in the business of exceeding expectations. He's in the business of blessing us abundantly, far beyond anything we deserve.

That day serves as a constant reminder that I don't have to have it all together to push forward. I don't have to be the best; I just need to put my needs out there and let God meet them. Put out what you've got, and you will be met with the rest every single time.

The Growing Season

Ecclesiastes 3:1–13

1 There is a time for everything,
and a season for every activity under the heavens:

2 a time to be born and a time to die,
a time to plant and a time to uproot,

3 a time to kill and a time to heal,
a time to tear down and a time to build,

4 a time to weep and a time to laugh,
a time to mourn and a time to dance,

5 a time to scatter stones and a time to gather them,
a time to embrace and a time to refrain from
embracing,

6 a time to search and a time to give up,
a time to keep and a time to throw away,

7 a time to tear and a time to mend,
a time to be silent and a time to speak,

8 a time to love and a time to hate,
a time for war and a time for peace.

9 What do workers gain from their toil? 10 I have
seen the burden God has laid on the human race. 11
He has made everything beautiful in its time. He has
also set eternity in the human heart; yet no one can
fathom what God has done from beginning to end. 12
I know that there is nothing better for people than to
be happy and to do good while they live. 13 That each
of them may eat and drink, and find satisfaction in
all their toil—this is the gift of God.

Often, we start out with grand plans for our lives, and things just don't go as planned. Life tends to happen, failures happen, and hard times come and go. The *good stuff*, though, happens in the living. The good stuff happens in the in-between.

I've been growing radishes in my garden for years. I started when Noah was three years old, seven years ago as I write this. And they were always terrible, bitter or so hot they were inedible. I'd fiddle with the soil and try again. When we moved, I restarted the garden. Failed radishes. Many other beautiful veggies grew, but never a tasty radish. We moved again, and again, no delicious radishes. This year, 2021, I came to a conclusion: *Stop growing radishes, Danielle. They never work out. Last year, they wouldn't even sprout, and the few that grew full-size tasted like hot soap.*

But something inside me encouraged me to give it another go. The seventh time is a charm!

Well, let me tell you—the first wave I picked today tasted like *heaven*. Crisp and full of watery, hot goodness. It took six growing seasons to achieve an edible radish. It took lots of reading and tinkering and patience. Seven years ago, I was thirty-two. A lot of living has happened since then. It's been a perpetual and continuous learning season.

Don't give up! Don't relent during your learning season. Don't yield during your grieving season. Even if you just keep failing, keep on! I promise you that the perfect radish isn't even the reward here. The reward is all that *living*, trying and trying again.

The perfect radish is just icing on the cake, a gentle reminder to never give up.

I don't think I'll ever look at a radish quite the same way. These are going to be a very victorious snack, with soft butter and crunchy salt. Never ever stop trying. Never ever wish away the growing season.

A Promise in the Blooms

Have you ever smelled a fresh-cut bouquet of peonies? The fragrance is soft yet powerful; some varieties almost have a punchy citrus note you just catch as you walk into a room filled with their perfume. Just a small, potted bouquet can transform the room it's in. Simply put, peonies are delightful.

A friend of mine asked me to attend a peony harvest with her recently. I'd never heard of such a magical thing! I told her I'd love to attend. The idea was that since the end of the season was approaching, this would be a final harvest capped off with a lovely luncheon. If you've ever seen a peony bush in real life, you know the stems bend over and touch the ground under the weight of the bloom, so they need to be cut and put in a vase immediately.

They are a flower meant to be cut. Their beauty and full glory are realized, for me, only once they've been cut from their parent plant and displayed for all to see inside the home. That's when the peony comes to life and shines.

I looked at that field and listened as the gardener said, "Why don't we start with twenty stems each, then we will go from there!"

Twenty stems? I was standing beside twenty other attendees, and there didn't appear to be twenty stems left out there. These plants looked as though it was truly the end of the season, not much to gather. But nevertheless, we started hunting for suitable blooms to cut. I was surprised to discover how easily I found blooms. From a distance, what looked too picked over turned out not to be at all. There were so many beautiful flowers left.

As we attendees picked and snipped, the field began to look almost bare. But each time I set out down the rows, I came upon more unopened blooms ready to be cut. With the weight of the other flowers removed, the stems picked themselves up to display even more buds. Through this cutting and gleaning process, the peony plants seemed almost to sigh in relief. And our arms were full of life and beautiful flowers! Now that the peonies had been cut, they could last a month longer in our homes. I wandered up and down the rows, smiling and watching the other guests cut their flowers.

Often, I find, time must pass before I see Jesus in a particular experience. I need to be removed for a bit from a situation to see that He was there working on my behalf the whole time. But on this day in the peony fields, almost immediately, I wandered away from my friend and was vividly aware how tenderly God had designed this magnificent plant. It needs to be cut to flourish. It needs the heavy blooms to be removed and shared to thrive.

I thought about the last ten years of my life and the loss and the struggle therein. Each bloom, it seemed, represented an area in my life that had needed to be cut. And though at the time it may have been painful or felt even unnatural, the truly challenging experiences of my life had been cut, processed, and shared, the glory in every case given back to the Lord. And in the process, I had reaped the benefit. I had been able to take my stems up off the floor to reveal more blooms and areas that needed to be cut for sharing. Each difficult experience opened the door to heal my own heart. I now see Jesus in nature. I can see His hand on our lives in the patterns and ways that plants grow and flourish.

After cutting my share of blooms that day, I wandered over to a tiny, beautiful orchard to eat lunch at a picnic table among apple and pear trees. It felt special. It was rural and simple and relaxing. Nothing fancy, just trees and flowers and boxed ham sandwiches. In the middle of all that, the blooms, the lunch, it took a lot of strength for me not to cry into my food.

There was a smiling woman with kind eyes setting up at a table nearby. She planned to show us how to create a stunning floral arrangement as we ate. As she began, it was hard to see the vision for the bouquet. Branches seemed just to jut out every side of the compote. I was beginning to think it might not look that good as she tucked big, thick branches into the floral wire. She had chosen flowers that didn't seem to go together. But as she arranged, a shape began to take form. She tucked and clipped and spoke, and the most creative, stunning shape simply emerged from her hands!

She paused just before finishing, and with wild-eyed excitement, she said, "I adore processing days." She went on to say that as a florist, she "processes" the flowers, removing thorns and excess foliage, cutting the stems on a diagonal to give the flowers the best chance at vase life. "I could spend days processing," she said wistfully.

I was floored. She adored the process of giving the flowers the best chance at vase life. My mouth was full of ham sandwich, and my heart was bursting. A ham sandwich doesn't seem too profound. But for me, ham reminds me of Minoela. The ham and Brie sandwich we served at our restaurant always remained a bestseller. Good bread, thinly sliced ham, and that gooey cheese—it was always satisfying and delicious. It was special. Nothing *fancy*, but pretty glorious.

Here we were, sitting in an orchard and learning about matters far more profound than merely arranging flowers. We were learning about life and treasuring the moment, all while eating ham sandwiches. I was reminiscing about the years I'd been living and reveling in the moments that seemed so clear now, in hindsight. There had been purpose in all these years. I keep seeing it, and I will continue to see it. There is purpose in our pain, in our grief, in our cuts, and in our losses. It's preparation to give us a better chance at living. I am keenly aware of it now. I am softer now, more willing to lean into the pruner's hands. We are going to thrive...as long as there are ham sandwiches. I think we can always pack a ham sandwich.

The whole of our lives isn't deemed "good" once we've arrived in the place we think we ought to. Our lives are good because we are alive and trying, drawing close to Jesus in the midst of the struggle. Life is good when we live together openhandedly, sharing our experiences and working to be better versions of who we were the day before.

Our lives are made for processing, the Lord tenderly removing our thorns and excess to give us the best chance at life. The words of this masterful florist were just what I needed to hear. The process of preparing was *far better* than the shaping and final arrangement. In the past ten years of my life—in this collection of moments—I am able to see how God has taken my mistakes, my pride, and my shortcomings and graciously forgiven, woven, and redeemed my story. When the storms of life come now, I know to lean into the waves and into Jesus, even if they are crushing. Because he's my only hope at making it through. Then, once the storm has cleared, though it may take a while for the tears to subside, I know I am a stronger me, better equipped and ready to share His goodness with others.

This life is meant for seasons of processing, preparing, and enduring. A honeybee works tirelessly to prepare and provide honey for the seasons to come. I'll take a life in process. I'll take a life facing the relentless wind. I'll take a life with Jesus. I pray that through all my stories, you can recall the past triumphs and trials in your own life in a way that softens you and tenderizes your heart. I pray that you can laugh and keep on going. I pray that you share and tell and go after your dreams boldly, but never forget to love *right now*, *right here*, imperfect and flawed and in spite of the tight coats of life and the extra baby weight. Don't let who you think you ought to be sway you from living fully just as you are. Take the bitter with the sweet, and remember who you are.

You were always there.

READING GROUP GUIDE

1. Of the stories in the book, which resonated most with you, and why?

2. Throughout the book, Danielle talks about some her most difficult moments. What difficult situation have you faced in the past year? What advice do you think Danielle would have given you about it?

3. Where does the fear of "losing yourself" come from? How do our expectations contribute to that fear?

4. Food is a way for us to connect with others. How can we make

these connections a part of our daily lives even when we're short on time and resources?

5. Thoughtful, reflective rest is emphasized throughout the book. What does a truly restful day look like to you? What obstacles do you contend with to achieve a day like that? Where, in your current schedule, could you take a moment to reflect when you don't have time to make a whole day of it?

6. Often, timing is out of our control. What does perseverance look like throughout the book? Can you think of an example from your own life where a key part of your success was timing? What does it take to be patient when you know your time is "not yet" and your efforts don't feel like they're paying off?

7. Lydia's casserole, fudge, pineapple mint, and garden strawberries are dishes and ingredients that remind Danielle of important people in her life. Is there a dish in your rotation that makes you think of someone special?

8. How does Danielle handle insecurity and impostor syndrome as a professional and as a mother?

9. In "The Lion Beside Me," Danielle reflects on loneliness and the strength and faith she relies on in her most isolated

moments. Who do you rely on for support? What will you do the next time you find yourself alone in a difficult moment?

10. Danielle challenges us to reconsider what makes a good life— not achieving our goals, but living with faith, effort, and gratitude. Did that surprise you? What aspects of your life shine forth when you think about it from this perspective?

A CONVERSATION WITH
THE AUTHOR

How did you decide to write *You Were Always There*? How did the experience differ from writing one of your cookbooks?

I've come to find over the years that writing is a form of therapy for me. When writing recipes, they must be very technical and precise. In writing stories about experiences I have had in life, I am able to heal through the writing. I started keeping notes on my phone for the feelings I was having. Then, late at night, those feelings became essays. When an essay was finished, it was this wonderful relief, not only for tucking something personal away as a diary entry but for helping me to see God's glory in what I had been through.

You talk about some very intimate and challenging parts of your life throughout the book. How did it feel to write about those moments? How did you take care of yourself during the process?

I didn't realize it before I started writing, but it ended up being difficult and also very freeing. Being able to relive certain memories further enforced the work Jesus has done in my heart and bring up areas to further pray through if they still stung. I really prayed over my heart and my family during that time. I was able to pray for Mike in a new way, and I didn't force things if they weren't flowing.

What similarities do you find between writing and cooking? Does one influence the way you approach the other?

Absolutely, especially when coming up with a new recipe. I find that writing exactly how feelings are coming up in my mind and sorting through it after feels the best for me. My favorite recipes are freestyle using fresh herbs and olive oil and taking a very relaxed approach to plating and cooking. Often the best recipes that come from my kitchen are ones where I had some chicken thighs and olives that needed to get used up, and a grilled lemon and tomato olive vinaigrette just happens. This is how I write. I never force it. If the inspiration isn't there, I will give it time, and then later, using the experiences from the day, sometimes I am able to come up with my very favorite stories focusing on hope.

You write so beautifully about the gifts we only see in hind-sight, especially when it comes to raising kids. Do you find it easier to appreciate the day-to-day moments with that in mind?

I do these days; I am grateful that even during tough experiences or very busy seasons I am able to pause and ask the Lord to guide me and help me be more present. It's something I am keenly aware of. We only have a certain amount of time, and I want to use that gift wisely.

What are your biggest challenges when developing new recipes or other new ideas? How do you combat them?

Sometimes I feel like something has already been done, so why make a new version? I am then quickly reminded that my version matters. Just as our stories matter. I'll jot down ideas and stories in notepads stashed around my home. Sometimes I'll flip back though and be inspired by something I wrote a year ago. I never stop scribbling.

Who are your biggest inspirations as a chef and writer?

The way Jamie Oliver approaches food greatly influenced who I am as a cook. And every grandmother in Europe and rural America. I am fascinated with artisanal foods and old ways of life in preserving and enjoying food. I like to take old ways and incorporate that slow way of living with our lifestyle now.

What books are on your bedside table right now?

Besides the four empty drinking glasses and my son's dirty cereal bowl I have an old *Bon Appétit* magazine, the Bible, and Frederick Douglass's biography. I am a huge history buff!

ACKNOWLEDGMENTS

One beautiful evening in Boston some years ago, I met a friend who changed my life. Talk of butterscotch pudding and purple tennis shoes made us fast friends and bonded us forever! Kelly Barrales-Saylor would later become one of my editors at Sourcebooks, and she introduced me to teams of people there who believed in my voice and message and who worked tirelessly to get that message out there in the world. Somehow, a kid who never did the best in school and who was always messing up found her place writing books. Sourcebooks has now published eleven of my books, and I'm forever grateful for that. Thank you for believing in me, Kelly B.

There has never been a moment during this project when I wasn't wholly supported. I can specifically remember crying out to the Lord for help in my writing a while ago, and shortly thereafter I was on the phone with Anna Michels, my editor. She said, "Well, I'd like to be that help." She faithfully believed that I could write this book, and she asked me to share in a way I don't think I could have without her push. Thank you, Anna.

Thank you to my sister, Jenny, who has been a constant source of support in every fashion of the word—not only throughout the writing of this book but as far back as I can remember. Whenever I've phoned Jenny, tears running down my face and proclaiming that I simply can't hack it, she's come to my rescue. She brings me Thai food and coffee and pep talks, and she's loved my children as her own. She's made my life lighter, more manageable. She is funny and beautiful and would give you anything she had, even if it was her last one. She has always been and continues to be my true-blue best friend.

And then there's Mike, a true companion and loyal friend, keeper of my dreams and a damn good editor. His sense of humor paired with his good nature and sly charm has always been there, even when I couldn't see it. Without his contribution to literally every achievement I've ever been proud of during our marriage, I'd have none of it. There would be no books without Mike, no Rustic Joyful Food, no Noah, no Milo. Mike's presence has been a gift in my life.

I also have to thank my mom and dad. Growing up, my parents didn't come from the greatest homes; they came from pain and abuse. So they were determined to give their kids a life full of grace, hope, and do-overs—all of which I touch on in these pages. Throughout the writing of this book, I can't even count how many times I called my mom for prayer. Along with my sister and husband, she is my best friend, and I know I get my robust work ethic from her. And without my dad, I'd never have the certainty that I could do anything I wanted, *right where I was*, no matter what. You don't need fancy things to make a life you love; you just need to love the life you've been given. His voice is in all we do at Rustic Joyful Food. He's the last to eat at dinnertime and the first to meet your needs. He's a good man and a hero.

To every person who said yes, who held court for us, who bought a book or attended a workshop, I thank you. Life is good when people surround us, and we are never alone thanks to our savior Jesus. Without God's gentle pursuit of my heart, I wouldn't know how to love well. He is everything in my life, my why and my hope. I want you to find the same hope in Jesus. He's open 24/7, ready and waiting.

And a special thank-you to these people, all of whom assisted in ways big and small, directly and indirectly, in the creation of this work: Sandra Stillwagon Westerman, Sandy Dunham, Cherie Wall, Kelli Bishop, Lisa Patterson, Jeff Hobson, Rachael Ray, Kelly Clarkson, Megan Barry, Casey Kopp, Alex Duda, Tracy Verna, Margaret Larson, Kate Huisentruit, Jeanette Donnarumma, Glenn Milley, Meredith Weintraub, Andrew Lear, Tracy Verna, Dominique Raccah, Brian Hovis, Alex Zennan, Anna Richter, Michaelan Mena, Dana Leavitt, Krystal Howard, Josh Dunn,

Jennifer Marrs, Sarah Lyons, Lauren Emerson, and Malia and Justin Isenhart.

ABOUT THE AUTHOR

Danielle Kartes is an author, food stylist, and recipe developer living in Seattle, Washington, with her husband, Michael, a photographer; and their two sweet sons. Together, the Karteses run their boutique food photography business, Rustic Joyful Food, and host food-styling workshops around the country. Danielle is a regular contributor on the hit daytime talk show *The Kelly Clarkson Show* and appears frequently on national television, speaking about joy and teaching how to cook simple, delicious food.